Best Climbs
Rocky Mountain National Park

Additional Climbing Titles by Stewart M. Green:

Best Climbs Moab
Best Climbs Denver and Boulder
Best Climbs Phoenix, Arizona
KNACK Rock Climbing
Rock Climbing Colorado
Rock Climbing Europe
Rock Climbing Utah
Rock Climbing Arizona
Rock Climbing New England

Visit the author's website: http://green1109.wixsite.com/ stewartmgreenphoto

Best Climbs
Rocky Mountain National Park

Karen Morris climbs through the Keyhole on Longs Peak.

PHOTO SPENCER SWANGER

Best Climbs
Rocky Mountain National Park

Over 100 of the Best Routes on Crags and Peaks

Second Edition

STEWART M. GREEN

FALCONGUIDES

GUILFORD, CONNECTICUT

Dedicated to the memory of my friend
Spencer Swanger (1940–2010)—mountaineer, adventurer,
husband, and father. Spence, we miss you. Just keep on climbing
and we'll see you on the other side of the mountain.

FALCONGUIDES®

An imprint of The Rowman & Littlefield Publishing Group, Inc.
4501 Forbes Blvd., Ste. 200
Lanham, MD 20706
www.rowman.com
Falcon and FalconGuides are registered trademarks and Make Adventure Your Story
is a trademark of The Rowman & Littlefield Publishing Group, Inc.

Distributed by NATIONAL BOOK NETWORK

Copyright © 2019 The Rowman & Littlefield Publishing Group, Inc.

Photos by Stewart M. Green except where indicated
Maps by The Rowman & Littlefield Publishing Group, Inc.

British Library Cataloguing in Publication Information available

Library of Congress Cataloging-in-Publication Data available

ISBN 978-1-4930-3933-3 (paperback)
ISBN 978-1-4930-3934-0 (e-book)

∞™ The paper used in this publication meets the minimum requirements of
American National Standard for Information Sciences—Permanence of Paper for
Printed Library Materials, ANSI/NISO Z39.48-1992.

Printed in the United States of America

The author and The Rowman & Littlefield Publishing Group, Inc. assume no
liability for accidents happening to, or injuries sustained by, readers who
engage in the activities described in this book.

WARNING

Climbing Is a sport where you may be seriously injured or die. Read this before you use this book.

This guidebook is a compilation of unverified information gathered from many different climbers. The author cannot ensure the accuracy of any of the information in this book, including the topos and route descriptions, the difficulty ratings, and the protection ratings. These may be incorrect or misleading, as ratings of climbing difficulty and danger are always subjective and depend on the physical characteristics (for example, height), experience, technical ability, confidence, and physical fitness of the climber who supplied the rating. Additionally, climbers who achieve first ascents sometimes underrate the difficulty or danger of the climbing route. Therefore, be warned that you must exercise your own judgment on where a climbing route goes, its difficulty, and your ability to safely protect yourself from the risks of rock climbing. Examples of some of these risks are: falling due to technical difficulty or due to natural hazards such as holds breaking, falling rock, climbing equipment dropped by other climbers, hazards of weather and lightning, your own equipment failure, and failure or absence of fixed protection.

You should not depend on any information gleaned from this book for your personal safety; your safety depends on your own good judgment, based on experience and a realistic assessment of your climbing ability. If you have any doubt as to your ability to safely climb a route described in this book, do not attempt it.

The following are some ways to make your use of this book safer:

1. Consultation: You should consult with other climbers about the difficulty and danger of a particular climb prior to attempting it. Most local climbers are glad to give advice on routes in their area; we suggest that you contact locals to confirm ratings and safety of particular routes and to obtain first-hand information about a route chosen from this book.

2. Instruction: Most climbing areas have local climbing instructors and guides available. We recommend that you engage an instructor or guide to learn safety techniques and to become familiar with the routes and hazards of the areas described in this book. Even after you are proficient in climbing safely, occasional use of a guide is a safe way to raise your climbing standard and learn advanced techniques.

3. Fixed Protection: Some of the routes in this book may use bolts and pitons that are permanently placed in the rock. Because of variances in the manner of placement, weathering, metal fatigue, the quality of the metal used, and many other factors, these fixed protection pieces should always be considered suspect and should always be backed up by equipment that you place yourself. Never depend on a single piece of fixed protection for your safety, because you never can tell whether it will hold weight. In some cases, fixed protection may have been removed or is now missing. However, climbers should not always add new pieces of protection unless existing protection is faulty. Existing protection can be tested by an experienced climber and its strength determined. Climbers are strongly encouraged not to add bolts and drilled pitons to a route. They need to climb the route in the style of the first ascent party (or better) or choose a route within their ability—a route to which they do not have to add additional fixed anchors.

Be aware of the following specific potential hazards that could arise in using this book:

1. Incorrect Descriptions of Routes: If you climb a route and you have a doubt as to where it goes, you should not continue unless you are sure that you can go that way safely. Route descriptions and topos in this book could be inaccurate or misleading.

2. Incorrect Difficulty Rating: A route might be more difficult than the rating indicates. Do not be lulled into a false sense of security by the difficulty rating.

3. Incorrect Protection Rating: If you climb a route and you are unable to arrange adequate protection from the risk of falling through the use of fixed pitons or bolts and by placing your own protection devices, do not assume that there is adequate protection available higher just because the route protection rating indicates the route does not have an X or an R rating. Every route is potentially an X (a fall may be deadly), due to the inherent hazards of climbing—including, for example, failure or absence of fixed protection, your own equipment's failure, or improper use of climbing equipment.

There are no warranties, whether expressed or implied, that this guidebook is accurate or that the information contained in it is reliable. There are no warranties of fitness for a particular purpose or that this guide is merchantable. Your use of this book indicates your assumption of the risk that it may contain errors and is an acknowledgment of your own sole responsibility for your climbing safety.

Rocky Mountain National Park Area

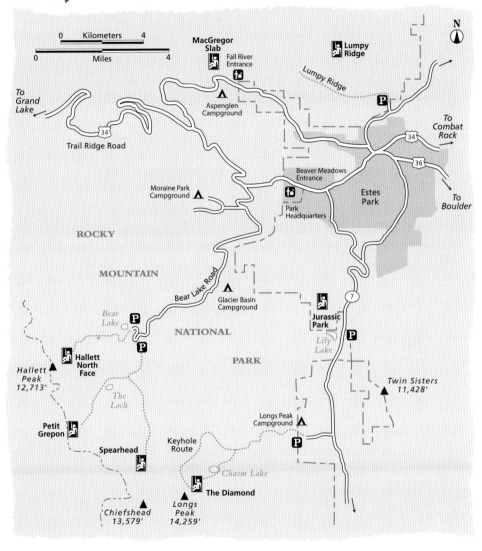

Contents

Introduction

Rocky Mountain National Park, Colorado's largest parkland, dominates the northern Front Range. It's a land of magical beauty—glacier-carved gorges, meandering rivers and rushing creeks, dense evergreen forests and sunny meadows, and herds of bighorn sheep, elk, and deer. But it's the skyscraping mountains and sharp granite cliffs that define the park for climbers and lovers of high places.

Lofty ragged peaks, sculpted by ancient glaciers, tower above the park's valleys and line the twisting Continental Divide, the spine of North America. The park includes 113 named mountain peaks above 10,000 feet, seventy-six over 12,000 feet, and nineteen over 13,000 feet, as well as Longs Peak, the park's high point at 14,259 feet above sea level.

Rocky Mountain National Park offers some of the best alpine rock climbing adventures in the United States. Numerous classic multi-pitch climbs ascend the high peaks and cliffs at this vertical sanctuary, including the standard *Keyhole Route* and routes on the sheer face of the Diamond on Longs Peak; the Northeast Face of Spearhead, the park's most beautiful mountain; the spired summit of the Petit Grepon; and the three vertical buttresses on Hallett Peak. Besides the alpine cliffs, the park's lower elevations host friendly granite crags at Lumpy Ridge and MacGregor Slab. Outside the park are numerous other venues, including wonderful sport climbing at Jurassic Park and Combat Rock.

Best Climbs Rocky Mountain National Park guides you to the area's very best climbs and cliffs. After climbing these classic routes, consider buying the comprehensive area guides, two by Bernard Gillett, and two by Richard Rossiter. In those four books you'll find lots of remote and untrammeled cliffs for other high-country trips. Some recommended venues not described here include Mount Meeker; Lower East Face and Chasm View on Longs Peak; Northwest Face of Chiefshead; Sharkstooth; Wham; more at Lumpy Ridge including Bookmark Pinnacle, The Bookmark, Left Book, and Bookend; and sport climbing at The Monastery.

When you climb at Rocky Mountain National Park, you're going to enjoy some of your best climbing days ever. You'll find granite walls glowing

> Rocky Mountain National Park boasts 113 named peaks over 10,000 feet, seventy-six topping 12,000 feet, nineteen over 13,000 feet, and one, Longs Peak, topping 14,000 feet. Longs Peak, Colorado's fifteenth-highest mountain, is the park's high point at 14,259 feet.

Ian Spencer-Green finds fun on *Stout Blue Vein* at Jurassic Park.

rusty red at sunrise; towering peaks etched against a cobalt vault of sky; lofty belay stances overlooking glaciated cirques; and summits that end where the sky begins. Standing on a summit, coiling your rope, you'll agree with Enos Mills, a climber and father of Rocky Mountain National Park, when he said, "Few experiences can put so much into one's life as to climb a mountain summit, and from among the crags and snows and clouds look down upon the beautiful world below."

Getting Around

Rocky Mountain National Park is easily accessed by major highways from Colorado's northern Front Range cities, including Denver, Boulder, Longmont, Loveland, and Fort Collins. From Denver and Boulder, follow US 36 to Estes Park. Denver is 65 miles away.

The park, open twenty-four hours a day year-round, has two entrances near Estes Park. The Beaver Meadows Entrance, west of Estes Park on US 36, leads to Moraine Park and Glacier Basin Campgrounds, the Bear Lake shuttle parking area, and the Glacier Gorge and Bear Lake trailheads. The Fall River Entrance enters the park northwest of Estes Park on US 34. It allows access to MacGregor Slab and Trail Ridge Road.

A fee is required to enter the park, except to climb on Longs Peak and Lumpy Ridge. Seven-day passes, an unlimited Rocky Mountain National Park annual pass, and the National Parks and Federal Recreational Lands Annual Pass can be purchased at the entrance stations.

All of the trailheads for the various cliffs are reached by road. In summer, however, the parking lots at the Glacier Gorge and Bear Lake trailheads fill quickly. If they are posted "full," park at the Park & Ride lot across from Glacier Basin Campground and take a free shuttle to both trailheads. Climbers shouldn't usually have a problem with parking, though, because you need to be parked and hiking by daybreak to avoid afternoon storms.

Climbing Seasons

Rocky Mountain National Park's weather conditions and temperatures vary dramatically. High elevations are cool and wet, while low elevations are drier and warmer. The best season for alpine climbs runs from June through August. May and September, depending on snow and weather conditions, can offer decent days on sunny cliffs. Expect cool days, with temperatures rarely above 70 degrees and dropping as low as 40 degrees, and regular afternoon thunderstorms. The storms, which quickly build over the mountains, can be severe with heavy rain, corn snow, and high winds. They're also often accompanied by lightning, the park's greatest climbing danger, and snow can fall on any summer day. Remember that the temperature at the Longs Peak summit is usually 30 degrees colder than in Estes Park. Bring a rain coat and extra clothes, and prepare for wet and cold conditions. Don't be afraid to retreat before bad weather comes. An early start is essential for all alpine climbs.

Lower-elevation crags—Lumpy Ridge, MacGregor Slab, Jurassic Park, and Combat Rock—are climbable all year, but the best weather is from April to October. The summer months are ideal, with mild daytime temperatures in the 70s and low 80s. The higher-elevation cliffs like Jurassic Park usually have cooler temperatures. Again, get an early start and be off the higher summits before the clockwork afternoon thunderstorms bring rain and lightning.

Climbing Regulations and Etiquette

Rocky Mountain National Park, administered by the National Park Service, has commonsense rules for minimizing the impact of climbers and hikers. These include not disturbing or damaging any natural feature, cultural resource, or park property; not removing plants, animals, rocks, fossils, or anything else; not picking, collecting, or damaging plants, including flowers; camping only in designated campgrounds; not building fires or gathering firewood; keeping vehicles on park roads and in designated parking areas; and not feeding, touching, or harassing wildlife. Dogs are not allowed in the backcountry, on trails, or at any cliff. They must be leashed in parking areas and campgrounds.

Several park regulations specifically address rock climbing. The use of power drills is prohibited in the park. Any bolt must be hand-drilled, although the use of bolts and fixed protection should be minimized. It's illegal to remove or clean vegetation from cracks or ledges and to disturb wildlife on the cliffs. Some cliffs might be seasonally closed for nesting raptors. Check the bulletin board at the Lumpy Ridge Trailhead parking area for Lumpy Ridge for closure updates. Littering is prohibited, so pick up after yourself, because your mother's not here to do it for you. It's

Longs Peak is on the Colorado state quarter, released in 2006. Then-governor Bill Owens picked the quarter design, saying it was a symbolic mountain image rather than a specific peak, thereby not offending those who wanted Pikes Peak on the quarter. It turns out, however, that quarter-designer Len Buckley based it on a photo of Longs Peak because he liked its rugged features.

not necessary to register to climb in the park, but it's a good idea to let someone know your plans and when you expect to return after climbing.

Climbers must obtain a permit to bivouac on or near their intended route. This permit system controls climber impact and keeps fragile ecological areas from overuse. Bivouac permits are obtained at the Wilderness Office, next to the Beaver Meadows Visitor Center, during business hours, seven days a week or by calling (970) 586-1242. Permits are issued year-round. Permits are issued if the site is more than 3.5 miles from the trailhead and the climb is more than four pitches long. Bivy rules include sleeping on rock or snow (not vegetation), being 200 feet from water and clear of rockfall, limiting your party to a maximum of four climbers, using only stoves, and not erecting tents, supported tarps, or shelters. Camping below tree line and fires are prohibited. Restricted sites, including Broadway, Chasm View, and Sky Pond, are heavily used areas that have environmental damage. Human waste is a serious problem at bivy sites. Bury your business beneath 4 to 6 inches of soil and heed the call of nature over 200 feet from water sources. You are strongly encouraged to carry and use a human waste disposal bag.

Climbing Rack and Extras

Most of the climbs in Rocky Mountain National Park require traditional climbing skills, including placing gear for protection and creating anchor systems for belays. While gear suggestions are included in route descriptions, what you carry on your rack is up to you. Study your proposed route and decide what you need to safely protect yourself when you climb. Most alpine climbs are complicated with lots of different-size cracks; make sure you bring enough gear— remember, the sin is never carrying too much gear, but not enough.

A standard rack for most of the park's climbs should include:

- Set of RPs
- One to two sets of wired nuts
- Several medium to large hexentric nuts
- Ten to fifteen quickdraws
- Six to twelve 2-foot slings
- Free carabiners
- Set of TCUs
- Set of cams to 3 inches
- Either a 165-foot (50-meter) or 200-foot (60-meter) rope

Some descents, like The Diamond's rappels, might require two ropes. Bring and wear a helmet. Loose rock abounds on the high cliffs, and a helmet saves your head. If you're climbing the long mountain routes, bring extra webbing and a knife to cut it for replacing old slings on rappel anchors. Long pants with reinforced knees are great for climbing cracks. Wear sturdy boots or approach shoes on the long backcountry hikes to your route. Bring a headlamp so you can see if you're benighted on a climb or on the hike out. A small GPS unit can keep you oriented, and a cell phone, if you can get service, could be a lifesaver in an emergency. Bring plenty of water, either in bottles or a hydration pack, or a water-purification system or tablets. Don't drink water from area streams; they all contain giardia.

When you climb, bring along the "Ten Essentials" to provide yourself with the basic necessities for survival should the unexpected occur:

1. Navigation (map, compass, GPS)
2. Sun protection (hat, sunscreen)
3. Insulation (layered clothing)
4. Illumination (headlamp, flashlight)
5. First aid supplies (Band-Aids, bandages, gauze, tape, tweezers, etc.)
6. Repair kit and tools (knife, duct tape, etc.)
7. Nutrition (extra food)
8. Hydration (extra water)
9. Emergency shelter (tarp, tent, sleeping bag, or emergency blanket)
10. Fire starter (necessary for life-threatening emergencies only)

Climbing Dangers and Safety

Rock climbing is dangerous. That's a fact. The perils of climbing, however, are usually overstated. The risks we take are the ones we choose to take. Everything we do as climbers, including placing gear, setting anchors, tying into the rope, and belaying, is to mitigate the dire effects of gravity and to minimize the danger of climbing. It's up to you to be safe when you're climbing. Be safety conscious and use the buddy system to double-check your partner and yourself.

Redundancy is the key to your personal safety. Always back up every

Over sixty people have died hiking and climbing on Longs Peak. About one person a year dies on the mountain. Most fatalities are from falls. Other deaths occur from lightning, exposure, hypothermia, heart attack, and in 1889, a gunshot. Many accidents happen on Lamb's Slide as well as on the *Keyhole Route*'s Narrows and Homestretch sections.

**Climbers toss rappel ropes down
The Diamond on Longs Peak.**
Photo Andrew Burr

important piece of gear with another and use more than one anchor at belay
and rappel stations. Your life depends on it. Beginner climbers are most vulner-
able to accidents. If you're inexperienced, hire a guide or take lessons. Always
use sound judgment when climbing, and respect the danger. Don't get on
climbs beyond your ability and experience. Remember that most accidents
happen because of climber error.

Objective dangers, as at most climbing areas, abound in Rocky Mountain
National Park. Watch out for loose rock as you climb. Loose flakes and boulders
are common on the high-altitude cliffs, particularly after freeze-thaw cycles
in winter. Also watch for rockfall from parties above you. Wear a helmet when
climbing and belaying. Use all fixed gear with caution. Some climbs still have
old pitons and bolts, and it's hard to determine how secure they actually are.
Always back up fixed gear with your own. Weather can be fickle. Afternoon
thunderstorms with heavy rain move in quickly; be prepared to bail off your
route if necessary. Watch for lightning on any of the mountain climbs or at
Lumpy Ridge.

Use the following ten tips to stay safe when you're out climbing on Rocky Mountain National Park's cliffs:

- Always check your harness.
- Always check knots.
- Always wear a helmet.
- Always check the rope and belay device.
- Always use a long rope.
- Always pay attention.
- Always bring enough gear.
- Always lead with the rope over your leg.
- Always properly clip the rope into carabiners.
- Always use safe and redundant anchors.

To learn more about climbing, including basic skills like creating anchor systems, placing gear, jamming cracks, rappelling, belaying, and tying knots, buy my comprehensive instructional book *Knack Rock Climbing,* co-authored with Ian Spencer-Green.

Map Legend

🛡70	Interstate	○	Town
🛡25	US Highway		City
🛡74	State Highway		Climbing Area
🛡170	County Road		Crag/Boulder
=====	Gravel Road		Cliff Edge
-----	Unimproved Road	▲	Mountain Peak
....	Trail	🅿	Parking
～	Waterway	⛺	Camping
	Lake/Reservoir	•—•	Gate
	Falls	🚶	Trailhead
	Glacier		Ranger Station
⌐ ⌐ ⌐	National Forest/ State Park Boundary		

Topo Legend

○	Natural gear belay stance
x	Single piece of fixed protection (bolt or piton)
xx	Fixed belay station

Climbing across The Narrows, an exposed ledge high on the *Keyhole Route* on Longs Peak.
PHOTO SPENCER SWANGER

1.

Longs Peak

Longs Peak, Colorado's fifteenth-highest mountain at 14,259 feet high, lords over Rocky Mountain National Park as its highest and most famous peak. Longs Peak dominates the park as well as the northern Front Range, its sharp visage visible from the rolling prairie and downtown Denver.

With its breathtaking beauty, towering 1,700-foot-high East Face, and lofty prominence, Longs Peak is a climber's mountain. Its easiest climbs up the *Keyhole Route* and the Loft Route are spectacular scrambling adventures, while its ridges and faces, including *Keyhole Ridge* and the sheer 945-foot-high Diamond, are some of America's best alpine rock climbs.

Climbing Longs Peak is serious business. Don't underestimate the peak, even on its easiest routes. The mountain is remote, with a long hiking approach and lots of loose rock

Longs Peak

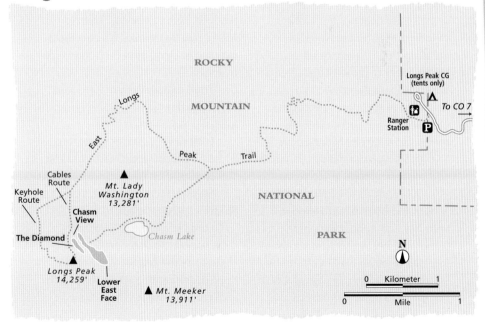

The Arapaho Indians, who lived in the valleys below Longs Peak, called it *Nesotaieux*, or "Two Guides," for its double summits and Mount Meeker. French fur trappers dubbed it *Les Deux Oreilles*, or "Two Ears."

and abrupt cliffs, and is subject to severe weather, which quickly builds over the peak. Use your best climbing judgment to evaluate changing conditions and weather, and always be prepared to retreat if necessary. Longs Peak is Colorado's most dangerous Fourteener, with at least one fatality occurring every year.

Leave early in the morning for every route. Most climbers depart before sunrise so they're on their route or the summit before afternoon thunderstorms, accompanied by lightning, occur. Severe weather usually comes from the west and often is unseen, especially on the East Face, before moving in. Also consider the high elevation of all the climbing routes. Climbing and hiking above 11,000 feet is always difficult, but more so if you're not properly acclimated.

The Longs Peak climbing season is from mid-May to mid-October, with July and August the prime climbing time. Expect sunny mornings and possible violent afternoon storms with heavy rain, corn snow or graupel, and lightning. Storms can

be brief showers or last all afternoon. May and June are fine for climbing, with stable weather periods. Consider all the climbs as technical outings and bring an ice axe, crampons, and rope. July and August are ideal for rock climbing on The Diamond, but severe weather often occurs in the afternoon. September and October are good for alpine routes, but expect snow above timberline and freezing temperatures. For current Longs Peak conditions, call the Rocky Mountain National Park information office at (970) 586-1206.

KEYHOLE ROUTE

This classic route involves moderate hiking on a trail and third-class rock scrambling. Expect exposure, steep terrain, and loose rock. There is not a trail to the summit; route-finding is required. It's a third-class climb from July to mid-September. No park fee is required to climb from the Longs Peak trailhead.

Trailhead elevation: 9,393 feet
Elevation gain: 4,776 feet from trailhead to summit
Distance: 13.2 miles round-trip
GPS coordinates: N 40.15.17 / W 105.36.55
Maps: USGS Longs Peak; Trails Illustrated #200 and #301

Longs Peak, one of Colorado's most popular Fourteeners, is usually climbed by the *Keyhole Route*. It is a third-class scramble above sheer cliffs, and it is generally free from snow early July to mid-September. During the rest of the year, the route is a technical mountaineering climb with snow and ice, requiring an ice axe, crampons, and rope.

The *Keyhole Route* is one of the most dangerous Fourteener climbs in Colorado. An average of one person a year dies while climbing Longs, often on the Keyhole Route, mainly from falls, lightning strikes, and exposure. The route requires scrambling across airy slabs and up steep gullies. Inexperienced climbers may need a belay on some sections. Use your best judgment to safely ascend the route.

The route, spiraling around Longs Peak, travels 6.6 miles from the trailhead to the summit, or 13.2 miles round-trip, making a long day. Begin before dawn (3 a.m. is a good start time) so that you climb the upper part of the route and then descend to a safe elevation before the daily thunderstorms begin. The scrambling upper parts can be difficult and dangerous if they're wet or covered with corn snow. Lightning also is an ever-present danger.

Be prepared for alpine conditions and bring the Ten Essentials, including warm clothing and rain gear. An ice axe, crampons, rope, and other gear may be needed. If you're coming from a low elevation, give yourself a few days to acclimate. Use caution when climbing the upper sections of the route and avoid climbing alone. Be especially careful not to knock rocks

down since other climbers are probably below you. It's a good idea to wear a helmet to protect your head. Keep an eye on the weather and don't be afraid to turn around in bad conditions.

Getting there: Longs Peak is west of CO 7, the Peak to Peak Highway. From Estes Park to the north, drive 9.2 miles south on CO 7 from its junction with US 36 to a right (west) turn to Longs Peak Ranger Station and Campground. From the south, drive 10.5 miles north on CO 7 from the junction of CO 7 and CO 72 and make a left turn to the ranger station. Drive a mile west to the Longs Peak trailhead. Parking can be a problem here; the lot usually fills in summer, especially on weekends. Overflow parking is along the road below the parking lot.

Enos Mills, the father of Rocky Mountain National Park, guided Longs Peak from his Longs Peak Inn. Mills climbed the mountain 297 times, including thirty-two ascents in August 1906. He first climbed Longs at age sixteen, made its first winter ascent in 1903, and made a solo descent of the East Face in 1903. "Climbing a high peak occasionally," Mills wrote, "will not only postpone death but will give continuous intensity to the joy of living."

Longs Peak Trailhead to Chasm Lake Trail Junction

The Route

Longs Peak Trailhead to Chasm Lake Trail Junction: The first 3.5-mile trail segment goes from the 9,393-foot-high Longs Peak trailhead (GPS: N 40.16.335 / W 105.33.408) to the Chasm Lake Trail junction east of Longs Peak. From the trailhead by the ranger station, hike west up East Longs Peak Trail. At a marked trail junction at 0.5 mile (GPS: N 40.16.483 / W 105.33.816), keep left on the main trail. The trail ascends through twisted limber pines in Goblins Forest (GPS: N 40.16.359 / W 105.33.204) at 1.2 miles, then switchbacks across a steep slope and crosses Alpine Brook on a log bridge. Keep left at the Jims Grove trail junction, 2.5 miles from the trailhead, and reach timberline. The Chasm Lake Trail junction (GPS: N 40.15.943 / W 105.35.552), at 11,550 feet, is at 3.5 miles. A privy is located here. Keep right at the junction on East Longs Peak Trail.

Chasm Lake Trail Junction to the Boulder Field

Longs Peak

The Diamond

The Keyhole

Boulder Field CG

Photo Doug Hatfield

Chasm Lake Trail Junction to the Boulder Field: The trail swings northwest from the junction and gently ascends the northeast flank of Mount Lady Washington for 1 mile (4.5 miles from the trailhead) to 11,994-foot Granite Pass (GPS: N 40.16.439 / W 105.36.316), a gap between Lady Washington and Battle Mountain. At the pass is another trail junction. Keep left on the main trail and hike 1.4 miles up a slope to the 12,400-foot-high Boulder Field (GPS: N 40.15.895 / W 105.36.853), a tumbled mass of boulders (5.9 miles from the trailhead). Hike through the boulders, passing a desolate camping area (permit only) and solar-powered toilets, to the southwest end of the Boulder Field at 12,800 feet.

The Keyhole

go left at Keyhole

Agnes Vaille
Hut

The Keyhole: Above the Boulder Field, clamber over boulders for 0.5 mile on a cairn-marked trail to the obvious Keyhole (GPS: N 40.15.614 / W 105.37.263), a pronounced notch in the northwest ridge of Longs Peak at 13,150 feet. The Keyhole (not to be confused with the False Keyhole farther south up the ridge) is the key to the route, allowing access from the east side of Longs Peak to the west side. The route becomes much more serious and demanding at the Keyhole, making it the turnaround point for many hikers unprepared for the terrain or weather. If the weather appears threatening, don't continue past the Keyhole. The wind is often very strong there. Below the Keyhole is the Agnes Vaille Shelter,

The Agnes Vaille Shelter, a beehive-shaped stone hut, sits below the Keyhole. Agnes Vaille, a well-known climber in the 1920s, died near here after making the first winter ascent of the East Face in January 1925. As she and her climbing partner, Walter Kiener, descended the North Face, Vaille fell 100 feet but landed in a snowdrift unhurt. She did, however, suffer from extreme fatigue after twenty-five hours of climbing and hypothermia in the frigid conditions and was unable to continue down. Kiener went for help, but when rescuers arrived, she had already died.

The Keyhole to the Trough

Photo Doug Hatfield

a beehive-shaped stone shelter that offers protection from storms.

The Keyhole to the Trough: The distance from the Keyhole to the summit is about a mile, but it is a time-consuming mile with lots of route-finding, exposure, and scrambling. From here the route spirals around the west and south sides of the mountain to the summit. The route is marked at crucial spots with painted yellow and red bull's-eyes. The bull's-eyes are the path of least resistance. If lost, you are likely in more difficult terrain. Retrace your steps until bull's-eyes are found again. Climb through the Keyhole to the west side of the northwest ridge and go left. Work up left from the Keyhole on ledges and slabs, up a V-Slot, and then across the Ledge, above the top of a slab. Special attention should be given to the V-Slot. This exposed and polished slab is the site of many accidents. Continue traversing across the face and after 0.3 mile from the Keyhole, reach the Trough, a steep gully that angles up right for 550 feet, at 13,300 feet.

Climbing the Trough

PHOTO DOUG HATFIELD

Climbing the Trough: The Trough is often filled with snow and may require crampons and an ice axe. If snow is still in the Trough, avoid it by keeping left on dry rock. The Trough is dry during summer. The gully has solid rock sections as well as rubble; watch for loose rock. Take care not to dislodge anything that may tumble onto climbers below. Wear a helmet to protect your head from klutzes above. Climb the Trough for 550 feet to 13,850 feet on the west ridge of Longs Peak, finishing with a 30-foot scramble up a rock wall and past a tricky chockstone (hardest part of the route) to a sudden airy view of Wild Basin to the south from a platform (GPS: N 40.15.259 / W 105.37.094).

The Narrows

The Narrows

Photo Doug Hatfield

The Narrows: From the top of the Trough, the route traverses the south face on an exposed ledge system called The Narrows, which traverses above a 300 foot cliff—it's not as bad as it looks. Cross the ledge for 300 feet, passing a couple of sections that narrow to 4 feet. It's usually dry with firm footing. Scramble up right on broken ledges and around a rib for another 400 feet to the base of the final section—The Homestretch.

The Homestretch to the Summit: The Homestretch, the easiest route through the summit cliffs, is a steep, 200-foot-long rock groove. Scramble up diagonaling cracks on steep slabs for 300 feet. Follow the painted markers to keep the difficulty at Class 3. If you stray off-route, the difficulty quickly increases. This section can be difficult and dangerous in bad weather or if there's snow. Above The Homestretch, scramble a few feet more onto the large, flat summit of Longs Peak (GPS: N 40.15.298 / W 105.36.908). Take some deep breaths. Eat your lunch. Take in the stunning views of surrounding peaks and the distant prairie shimmering in the afternoon sun. Don't forget to record your achievement in the summit register, along with the thousands of other climbers that have climbed to the fifteenth-highest summit in Colorado. If you want to stand on the actual high point, you'll have to scramble atop the obvious big boulder.

Descent: Reverse the route to descend. Novices sometimes freeze up before downclimbing the steep and exposed Homestretch. After leaving the Trough, pay attention to the traverse across the Ledge to make sure that at its end, you climb down to the Keyhole. Some returning parties mistake a higher notch called the False Keyhole for the real thing. While on top, keep an eye on the weather. If thunderstorms are building, start down

The Homestretch to the Summit

to summit

The Homestretch

Photo Doug Hatfield

Although a couple of parties claimed to have climbed Longs Peak, the first verifiable ascent (not including previous Native American ascents) was by a party of seven in 1868. The leaders of the ascent were Major John Wesley Powell, the one-armed explorer who made the first descent of the Green and Colorado Rivers, and William N. Byers, founder and editor of the *Rocky Mountain News*. The other climbers were Jack Sumner, W. H. Powell, and three college students—L. W. Keplinger, Samuel Garman, and Ned E. Farrell. They climbed Longs from Wild Basin, to the south.

immediately, before rain and lightning comes. The upper route sections are treacherous when wet or snowy.

KEYHOLE RIDGE

This excellent route follows the spectacular and exposed northwest ridge of Longs Peak from the Keyhole to the summit. *Keyhole Ridge* (II 5.6) makes a great technical summit route, is a good alternative to the standard *Keyhole Route,* and offers fun climbing on perfect granite. The route, requiring both commitment and route-finding, is usually done in five to seven roped pitches depending on conditions and experience. Some pitches are easily simul-climbed. Expect about 1,500 feet of technical climbing. Get an early start and climb fast to avoid afternoon storms—*Keyhole Ridge* is not a good place to be in a lightning storm. **Rack:** Sets of Stoppers and Camalots to #3.

Keyhole Ridge

Majka Burhardt leading the classic
Keyhole Ridge **on Longs Peak.**
PHOTO TOPHER DONAHUE

The Route

Keyhole to False Keyhole: Begin by hiking almost 7 miles from the Longs Peak trailhead to the Keyhole (GPS: N 40.15.614 / W 105.37.263) and the start of the *Keyhole Route*. From the Keyhole, scramble left (south) for 600 feet on an exposed rising ramp and ledge system (4th class) on the east side of the rocky northwest ridge and above a slab to the False Keyhole, a wide notch in the ridge.

False Keyhole to Upper Notch: Climb the easy ridge above the False Keyhole to a gendarme (5.0) with steeper rock. Climb an easy ramp (4th class) on the left (east) to pass the gendarme. When the ramp ends, climb straight up to the top of the gendarme and the ridge crest (5.4). Descend 10 feet down the west side of the ridge to a ledge system. Scramble up the ledge (4th class) and then slabs to the base of the next steep ridge section and the last notch in the ridge. Watch that you don't dislodge loose rocks onto the standard hiking route below.

Upper Buttress: Scramble up an easy ramp on the left (east) side of the ridge to the base of a steep buttress and belay. For a harder pitch, climb an obvious crack (5.6) straight up. Or continue up the narrowing ramp until it's possible to climb directly up excellent granite (5.5) to the ridge crest.

Upper Ridge: Follow the excellent and airy upper northwest ridge (3rd class) to the summit. Pass a section of large blocks on the right (west) side of the ridge, then climb the long, gently rising ridge to the summit of Longs Peak.

Descent: The easiest descent is down the *Keyhole Route*.

THE DIAMOND

The Diamond, an east-facing cliff above 13,000 feet, is one of America's most spectacular alpine big walls. The 900-foot-high wall is the centerpiece of the glacier-excavated East Face of Longs Peak. The Diamond is a climbing paradise, with perfect granite split by vertical cracks and studded with crisp edges.

Diamond climbing is serious business—expect an adventure or a possible epic. The approach is long, loose, and dangerous. The routes are

Timberline marks the highest elevation at which trees can live. Enos Mills called it "the line of battle between the woods and the weather." Wind-blasted stands of spruce and fir, called krummholz (German for "crooked forest"), form miniature forests along timberline. Tree growth is slow in the cold temperatures, harsh winds, and short growing season. A 200-year-old krummholz tree might be only 4 inches in diameter and 4 feet tall.

The National Park Service pro-hibited climbing The Diamond in the 1950s. In 1959 park service director Conrad Wirth barred "stunt and daring trick climbing" with The Diamond in mind. By 1960 a chorus of climbers prodded the park into new regulations with stringent requirements, including com-petency and a rescue team ready to pluck victims from the wall. Applications were sent to climbers who had previously requested permission to climb the face. Colorado climbers were unable to put together a team, so the first approved application fell to Californians David Rearick and Bob Kamps. They picked out an obvious directissima and began their ascent on August 1. The pair climbed the wall, emerging on the summit three days and eleven rope-lengths later, and descended to find themselves heroes in the national media and feted in an Estes Park rodeo parade.

The climbing season runs from mid-June to late September.

Quick parties climb The Diamond in a day, hiking before dawn to the wall's base in two or three hours. Add another six to ten hours of climbing and another three to four hours to descend and hike back to the car. Allow extra time to figure out the approach, climb, and descent routes. An option to a one-day ascent is to hike up the afternoon before and biv-ouac at Chasm View or on Broadway. With an early start you'll get sun and warmth while climbing. Also consider the high altitude—climbing above 13,000 feet is difficult, and even more so if you're not acclimated. After-noons, after the sun leaves the face, can be cold. Severe weather comes from the west and is unseen until it's on the face. The weather changes quickly. Expect afternoon thunder-storms accompanied by lightning.

All the routes begin on Broadway, a ledge system below The Diamond. Use caution when traversing Broad-way. Fatalities and accidents have occurred to unroped climbers on it. There are only a few bivouac sites on Broadway, and the park limits the number of climbers permitted to stay overnight. Obtain a bivy permit at the Longs Peak Ranger Station.

Getting there: Drive 7 miles south from Estes Park on CO 7 and turn right (west) past mile marker 9 toward Longs Peak Ranger Station and Camp-ground and the Longs Peak trailhead.

steep, exposed, and subject to severe weather. The descent routes are hard to find in the dark, bordered by snow-fields, and covered with rubble. The Diamond receives only morning sun.

Longs Peak East Face Overview

Drive a mile and park at a designated lot for the Longs Peak Trail (GPS: N 40.16.335 / W 105.33.408). The lot fills early on summer weekends. Look for overflow parking areas along the road below the parking lot. Hike west on East Longs Peak Trail to a major fork at 3.5 miles. The left fork continues to Chasm Lake, while the right fork heads to the *Keyhole Route*. The Diamond can be reached from both trails.

Approaches

The best and easiest approach to The Diamond is from Chasm Lake and the *North Chimney*. The climb up *North Chimney* is also the busiest and most dangerous approach. Watch for falling rock and ice from above. Be careful climbing below other parties that might be hauling a pack, which can knock rocks down on you. Wear a helmet. It's possible to climb *North Chimney* without a rope, but most parties rope up for some or all of the route. Conditions can be icy. Several fatalities have occurred on the *North Chimney*. There are lots of ways to climb *North Chimney;* the described line is best when it's dry.

From the Longs Peak trailhead (GPS: N 40.16.335 / W 105.33.408), hike uphill for 3.5 miles to the Chasm Lake Trail junction east of Longs Peak. Take the Chasm Lake Trail to the left and hike a mile west to Chasm Lake.

Pass the lake along its north side, cross a boulder field, and climb Mills Glacier below the lower wall. Scramble to the base of *North Chimney,* a deep cleft in the Lower East Face. This 500-foot-high loose gully system is directly below *D1.*

North Chimney Approach: (5.5) 3 to 4 pitches. Scramble up Mills Glacier to the base of the chimney system. The driest route climbs slabs and corners left of the gully. If snow is in the gully, kick steps up it to a huge chockstone. Pass it on the left and continue up left to a ledge and then to another loose ledge. Climb cracks and corners up right to Broadway. Traverse up left across Broadway above *North Chimney* on loose rock (5.3) to the base of the D1 Pillar. All the described Diamond routes are to the left (south) from here. Use caution when climbing, and watch for wet loose rock and climbers above knocking rocks down. Snow fills the gully in June, requiring an ice axe.

Chasm View Approach: Alternatively, approach Broadway from the north. Hike up the Longs Peak Trail to the Boulder Field. Past the camping site, go left and boulder-hop south to Chasm View, a

13,529-foot overlook at a notch north of The Diamond. Make three double-rope rappels from fixed anchors to Broadway. Traverse south on Broadway to your route. After climbing The Diamond, return to Chasm View by descending the North Face.

Descents

The routes (except the *Yellow Wall*) all end on Table Ledge, a horizontal crack and ledge system on the upper face. The preferred descent is to hike to the summit and descend the North Face. This is as fast as The Diamond rappel route and is easier in bad weather.

North Chimney

Exit off the routes by traversing left on Table Ledge to *Kiener's Route*. Scramble up *Kiener's* (3rd class) to the summit. Scramble down the peak's North Face along the old *Cables Route*, descending rocky slopes and snow-fields. At the top of a cliff band, locate large eyebolts and make either a two-rope rappel or two single-rope rappels to the Boulder Field. Check out the North Face descent in daylight before attempting it; don't try it in the dark. From the cliff base, scramble down to the Longs Peak Trail. You can also descend the standard *Keyhole Route,* but it is difficult to follow in bad weather and darkness if you're unfamiliar with it. Its advantage is that it requires no rappels or technical climbing. Follow paint splotches down the route on the peak's northwest side.

Alternate Diamond Descent:
An alternative descent is to rappel The Diamond's left (south) side above *D7.* The rappel anchors can be hard to find the first time, and the rappels get backed up on busy days. Allow at least two hours to rappel if you're unfamiliar with the rappel route. Begin from Table Ledge or below Table Ledge directly above *D7.* Make a 30-foot rappel from Table Ledge to anchors, then five double-rope rappels to Broadway from bolt anchors located near *D7.* Scramble north on Broadway and make another four rappels (100 feet, 150 feet, 150 feet, 150 feet) down the *Crack of Delight* to

the wall's base. These bolted rappels begin directly below the *Casual Route* and the D1 Pillar. Alternatively, make three double-rope rappels from fixed anchors down *North Chimney.*

1. Pervertical Sanctuary (IV 5.10d) Excellent and popular with varied crack climbing. The route ascends a crack system on the far left edge. Scramble south across Broadway and set the first belay right of a snow patch on a ledge below a crack system and right of the Obelisk, a dihedral on the Diamond's left side. **Pitch 1:** Climb broken cracks and then move up right to the left side of a mitten-shaped formation. Continue up the left dihedral (5.9) on the Mitten to a belay ledge on top. 185 feet. **Pitch 2:** Climb a blocky left-facing corner (5.9) to a stance on the right. **Pitch 3:** Work up a crack system to a small roof. Face climb left (5.9) past an old bolt, then move right up a flake to a ledge right of the Obelisk column. Combine pitches 2 and 3 with a 60-meter rope. **Pitch 4:** Start off the ledge's right side. Jam a strenuous 1.5-inch crack (5.10c) for 50 feet. Continue up the splitter for another 50 feet to a perch on a wedged block. **Pitch 5:** Continue up a sustained 4-inch crack (5.10a) with hand and fist jams. Jam a corner (5.8+) to a belay atop the Obelisk. **Pitch 6:** From the belay's right side, jam a steep finger crack (5.9) in a corner to a belay on Table Ledge. Finish by scrambling up left on easy rock to *Kiener's Route* and follow it to the summit. If you plan to rappel, scramble right on Almost Table Ledge to the first rap station. **Rack:** Sets of Stoppers and Camalots to #4 with doubles from #1.5 up; a #5 Camalot useful.

2. Ariana (IV 5.12a) Excellent route with exposure, clean granite, and sustained jamming. Begin right of a snow patch on a ledge above the south end of Broadway. This is reached by a traverse (4th class) up left from the base of #4, *Yellow Wall*. **Pitch 1:** Face climb above the belay (5.11a) past three bolts, then up a narrow left-facing corner (5.10b) to the bottom right side of the Mitten. Finish up a right-facing corner to the Mitten's thumb. The next two pitches climb *Pervertical Sanctuary* to the belay stance opposite the Obelisk's base. **Pitch 2:** Climb a blocky left-facing corner (5.9) to a stance on the right. **Pitch 3:** Climb a crack system to a small roof. Face climb left (5.9) past an old bolt, then move right up a flake to a ledge right of the Obelisk, a dihedral on the Diamond's south edge. **Pitch 4:** Above the belay is a 1-inch crack that is 5 feet from the Diamond's left edge. Jam the well-protected, sustained finger crack (pumpy 5.12a) to a semi-hanging belay on a sloping ledge to the right. **Pitch 5:** Step back left and continue jamming the steep crack (5.11c) in a right-facing corner to a large belay ledge. **Pitch 6:** Finish up *Pervertical Sanctuary* to Table Ledge. From the

The Diamond—Left Side

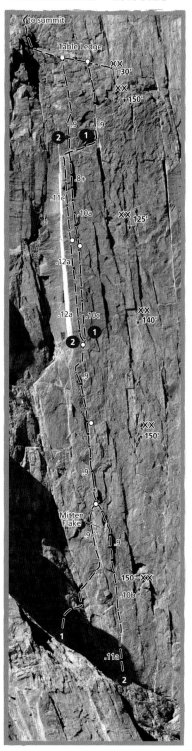

Nick Berry climbs cracks on *Ariana,* one of The Diamond's best climbs. PHOTO ANDREW BURR

right side of the ledge, jam a steep finger crack (5.9) in a corner to a belay on
Table Ledge. Finish by scrambling up
left on easy rock to *Kiener's Route* and
follow it to the summit. If you plan to
rappel, scramble right on Almost Table
Ledge to the first rap station. **Rack:**
Double set of Stoppers with extra
small and medium sizes, set of cams
from a #.3 Alien to a #3.5 Camalot, two
200-foot (60-meter) ropes.

3. D7 (V- 5.11d or 5.7 C2) Excellent
with easy clean aid or difficult free
climbing. The free crux is short and
well protected. Climb it at 5.10 C1
with minimal aid. Begin down right
of *Ariana* on a ledge/ramp (4th class)
below a left-facing corner that is 150
feet south of the Broadway bivy cave.
Scramble to the ledge and belay.
Pitch 1: Climb the left-facing corner
(5.9) for 70 feet to a good ledge on
the right. Continue up a crack (5.9) to
a belay ledge. 165 feet. **Pitch 2:** Climb
a left-facing corner for 40 feet and
then follow thin corners and cracks
(5.9) to a ledge. **Pitch 3:** Continue up
the widening crack system (5.10a).
If the crack is wet, face climb on the
left (5.10a). Belay on a sloping ledge
to the right, next to the *Yellow Wall*.
Pay attention to the start of pitch 4 to
avoid the wrong crack system. Don't
go straight up an obvious crack to the
left. This is *D Minor 7*. **Pitch 4:** Move
right from the belay and climb a shallow right-facing corner. Face climb
and stem the corner (5.9/5.10) to a

belay stance below thin, left-leaning
double cracks. **Pitch 5:** Sustained
moves work up the bulging parallel
cracks (5.11d for 15 feet) to a stance.
Climb another thin crack crux (5.11b)
to a small stance. 130 feet. **Pitch 6:**
Climb a thin crack (5.11a) above the
belay. It widens and leads to easier
rock (5.8) and Almost Table Ledge. A
set of rap anchors is just left if you're
rapping the face. **Pitch 7:** Climb up
left (5.8) for 40 feet to Table Ledge.
Scramble left across Table Ledge to
Kiener's Route and continue to the
summit. **Rack:** Double set of Stoppers, double set of Camalots to #3 and
single #3.5 and #4.

4. Yellow Wall (V 5.11a) Classic
route with sustained climbing, solid
rock, and lots of exposure. Begin 60
feet south of the Broadway bivouac
cave. Scramble up a ramp (3rd class)
below a narrow left-facing corner. The
original start aided this corner (A3 or
5.11a). **Pitch 1:** Face climb up flakes
(5.7) for 70 feet right of the corner,
then work left to a ledge atop the corner. Continue up a thin finger crack
(5.9) for 60 feet to a belay stance on
the left. 130 feet. **Pitch 2:** Climb a thin
crack (5.9+) to a small ledge. 130 feet.
Pitch 3: Climb a thin crack (5.10a) to a
hard corner (5.10a) that is often wet.
At the top, make tricky face moves
(5.10c) left to another crack system
and belay on a narrow ledge shared
with *D7*. 130 feet. **Pitch 4:** Layback a
shallow left-facing corner above the

The Diamond—Central Sector

right side of the ledge. Continue up right (5.8) under the obvious *Black Dagger* off-width crack, past a possible belay stance, and into a thin, right facing, red dihedral (5.9) Belay at a stance just right of an off-width crack. **Pitch 5:** Climb a corner up right to a hard-to-protect face traverse (5.11a R) that heads up right on flakes to a thin corner (5.10a). Climb the corner to the *Casual Route*'s large dihedral. Belay here or continue 40 feet up the dihedral (5.6) to the 4-foot-wide *Yellow Wall* bivy ledge. Protection is RPs and small Stoppers. To avoid this pitch, climb *Forrest Finish* (the route's natural line). **Pitch 6:** Shared with *Casual Route.* Stem between two opposing corners (5.9+) above the right side of the ledge and enter a chimney (5.8). Climb up left past a fixed piton in a thin crack, then over a bulge (5.10a), and belay at Table Ledge crack. Exit left to the rappels and *Kiener's* here to avoid the upper two pitches. **Pitch 7:** Traverse right on Table Ledge crack for 15 feet. Climb exposed cracks (5.10c) to a large right-facing dihedral. Belay on a small ledge on the right side of an overhang. **Pitch 8:** Climb a chimney (5.9) up the dihedral to a belay. Scramble up easy rock to the top of the wall. **Rack:** Sets of RPs, Stoppers, TCUs, and Camalots to #3.5.

5. Forrest Finish (5.10b) Two pitches from the *Yellow Wall* to Table Ledge. The *Forrest Finish* is a direct finish to the *Yellow Wall,* avoiding its 5.11 face

climbing. To start, climb the first four pitches of the *Yellow Wall* and belay at a stance right of an off-width crack. **Pitch 1:** Climb a wide crack to an off-width section (5.10a). Above, work up another off-width (5.10b), then climb up right (5.7) to a belay on the left side of the *Yellow Wall* bivy ledge. **Pitch 2:** Traverse left to the crack system and jam a crack up a clean face (5.10b) to a stance. Layback the

Duncan Ferguson and Chris Reveley free-climbed the easiest Diamond route in 1978, climbing a traverse and then up a dihedral to Table Ledge. Ferguson called the route *The Integral* or *The Old Man's Route.* That same summer, Charlie Fowler visited Ferguson at Komito Boots in Estes Park. Duncan told Charlie that his new route "would be a really secure thing to solo." The next weekend, Fowler scrambled to Broadway and launched solo up the new route just before sunrise. He audaciously soloed the airy traverse and then jammed secure cracks to the *Yellow Wall* crux, where he clipped a sling to a piton to protect himself. Later, when asked about the route, Charlie said it was "casual," giving the route its current name— the *Casual Route.*

strenuous crack (5.10a) and finish up a chimney to Table Ledge. Scoot left to the rappels and descend.

6. Casual Route (IV 5.10a) The easiest and most popular Diamond route. Expect excellent climbing with good protection and exposure. Pitches 3 and 4 are wet in June. Begin on Broadway below a corner just south of the upper rappel anchors for *North Chimney*. **Pitch 1:** Climb a left-facing corner (5.5) in the middle of the D1 Pillar, a large pillar below *D1*'s obvious crack. Continue up cracks on the buttress face. Belay at an alcove on the pillar's left side or climb to a stance left of the pillar's top. **Pitch 2:** The flakes traverse offers route-finding problems. Don't begin the traverse too low and or you'll find 5.10 face climbing with no pro and a possible serious fall. Jam a finger to hand crack (5.9) above the belay to a stance. Face climb up left on a rising traverse using flakes and edges (5.6 and 5.7) to a semi-hanging belay beneath a right-facing dihedral. 100 feet. **Pitch 3:** Climb a chimney (5.8) and then jam cracks past a sloping ledge (holds snow early in the season). More cracks lead up the dihedral's left wall (5.6/5.7) to a small belay ledge. **Pitch 4:** Jam a hand crack up the steep dihedral (5.8+) to a belay niche near the top of the dihedral. **Pitch 5:** Finish up the dihedral (5.7/5.8) to a belay on the *Yellow Wall* bivy ledge on the left. **Pitch 6:** From the ledge's right side, stem up exposed, opposing corners (5.9+). Squeeze up a chimney (5.8), jam a thin crack, and reach over a bulge (5.10a). Belay at the Table Ledge crack. This pitch is shared with the *Yellow Wall*. **Pitch 7:** Hand traverse left (5.7/5.8) along the horizontal crack. After 30 feet the crack widens. Jam it and traverse up left along Table Ledge to *Kiener's Route* and belay. Finish up *Kiener's* to the summit or rappel The Diamond. **Rack:** Double set of Stoppers, set of TCUs, double set of Camalots from #.5 to #3, six runners, and six quickdraws. Fixed pitons are found. A 200-foot (60-meter) rope is useful and shortens the climbing time by combining pitches.

Spearhead

2.

Spearhead

Spearhead perches above Glacier Gorge, an alpine basin flanked by ridges and cliffs, carpeted with meadows and forests, and dotted with lakes. The Spearhead lifts its pointed 12,575-foot-high summit above an 800-foot-high northeast face. This granite wall, dwarfed by surrounding peaks, is climber friendly, seamed with vertical cracks and dihedrals, and covered with incut handholds and flakes. Numerous great climbs up to nine pitches long ascend the concave wall, offering superb climbing in a remote setting.

Spearhead is the high point of a long ridge that juts north from Chiefshead. The pyramid-shaped northeast face is broken by several features. A horizontal grassy ledge—Middle Earth—splits the lower wall. The Eye of Mordor is a north-facing dihedral above Middle Earth, and Syke's Sickle is a crescent-shaped corner below the summit. A snowfield drapes along the wall's base in June.

Spearhead's climbing season runs from June through September. The wall receives lots of summer sun. Most routes are day climbs, but a limited number of bivouac permits are available for overnight camps below the wall. The permits are available at the Backcountry Office, next to the Beaver Meadows Visitor Center. Objective dangers include thunderstorms, snow and sleet, lightning, loose rock, and climbers above you. To avoid crowds, avoid the weekends.

Getting there: Reach Spearhead from the Glacier Gorge trailhead on Bear Lake Road. Drive west from Estes Park on US 36 into Rocky Mountain National Park. Turn south on Bear Lake Road past the Beaver Meadows Entrance Station and drive to a parking lot at Glacier Gorge trailhead a mile before the road's end at Bear Lake (GPS: N 40.310491 / W -105.640419). Get there early or walk the 0.5-mile trail down from the larger Bear Lake parking lot, or take the free shuttle from the Park & Ride lot across from Glacier Basin Campground. Hike south on Glacier Gorge Trail for 6 miles and two hours to Spearhead. The trail intersects North Longs Peak Trail at 1.4 miles. Keep right and in 0.5 mile turn south toward Mills Lake. The trail climbs steeply 0.6 mile to the lake and continues south along the east shore another 0.4 mile to Jewel Lake. It then continues up the forested floor of Glacier Gorge for another 1.8

Peggy Donahue climbing the *Northeast Ridge* of Spearhead.
PHOTO TOPHER DONAHUE

Rocky Mountain National Park—The High Peaks

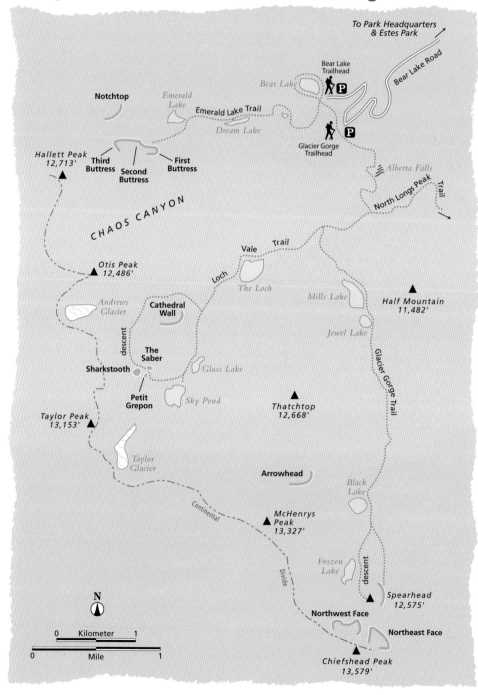

miles to 10,620-foot Black Lake (GPS: N 40.265563 / W -105.640081). Hike up steep slopes below a cliff band east of the lake and enter the upper basin below Spearhead. Follow a trail through meadows and across bedrock to the wall's base (GPS: N 40.256991 / W -105.637589).

Descent: Two descents from Spearhead's summit. Descend scree slopes, loose rock, and short cliff bands on its northwest face. At the base, hike around the Northeast Ridge and return on the access trail.

Layton Kor owned Rocky Mountain National Park in the 1960s. Layton made the second ascent of The Diamond via the first ascent of the *Yellow Wall* in 1962. He made the first one-day ascent of The Diamond up *D1* with Royal Robbins in 1963 and then two days later did the first ascent of *Jack of Diamonds*, again with Royal. Layton made the first winter ascent of The Diamond with Wayne Goss via the *Enos Mills Wall* in 1967. He also did the first ascent of many routes on Chasm View Wall and the Lower East Face on Longs Peak, as well as new routes on Hallett Peak, Sharkstooth, the Northwest Face of Chiefshead, and Lumpy Ridge. We're still climbing in your footsteps Layton!

Alternatively, scramble southwest across ledges to the saddle between Spearhead and Chiefshead and then scramble east down ledges (4th class) and a ramp to the basin. Watch for cliff bands, couloirs, snow patches, and loose rock, and prepare for routefinding.

1. Sykes Sickle (III 5.9+) Classic and excellent. Expect moderate climbing, good protection, and a thrilling finish. Get an early start to avoid afternoon thunderstorms on the summit slabs. The route follows an obvious sickle-shaped arch on the upper wall. Begin at the base below double crack systems directly below the Sickle and right of some streaked overlaps. **Pitch 1:** Climb the left of two parallel cracks (5.7) to a belay. 80 feet. **Pitch 2:** Continue up corners (5.4) to a terraced ledge above Middle Earth. Combine the first two pitches with a long rope. **Pitch 3:** Climb up left on easy terrain to a belay ledge. **Pitch 4:** Face climb (5.6) up right on flakes and cracks to a belay ledge at the base of a left-leaning dihedral system. **Pitch 5:** Jam cracks (5.7) up the dihedral to a belay below the Sickle. Alternatively, climb flakes on the face left of the dihedral (5.7) to the belay. **Pitch 6:** Squeeze up a flared chimney (5.7) on the left side of the Sickle and then traverse up right to an exposed ledge directly below a notch in the large roof above. The chimney is often wet. **Pitch 7:** Technical crux. Climb a

Spearhead

4th class to summit
descend 4th class ledges to south
descend talus on west side
.7
.6
.6 slot
.9+
.5
.6
.7 chimney
.5
.5
.7
.7
4th class
.3
.6
.4
.5 chimney
.4
.7
1
2

crack to the notched roof. Stem and pull over (5.9+) past fixed pitons with exposed moves. This section can be wet in early summer. Step left into a crack and climb up left to a belay stance. The hard roof move is easily aided. **Pitch 8:** Psychological crux. Traverse delicately right 35 feet across a polished slab (5.7) to a fixed pin and bolt. Climb up right on easier rock to a short corner and the summit ridge. **Rack:** Sets of Stoppers, TCUs, and Camalots to #3.5 or #4; 200-foot (60-meter) rope.

2. North Ridge (III 5.6) Outstanding classic route—one of the park's best long moderates. Expect fun climbing, lots of exposure, and plenty of variations and route-finding problems. The lower pitches are easily simul-climbed or can be strung together with a long rope. Most pitches as described are 130 to 150 feet long. Begin by scrambling up and around the Northeast Face to a dark chimney/cleft below the left side of the broad *North Ridge*. Also look for an obvious groove/slot above a lower slab. **Pitch 1:** Climb up left, passing beneath the chimney, and edge up left across the slab. Climb back right to the groove/slot and belay. **Pitch 2:** Stem up the groove and chimney (5.5) and belay below a tight dihedral. **Pitch 3:** Fun climbing leads up the V-shaped dihedral (5.4) to a right-facing dihedral. Belay on a ledge to the right. **Pitch 4:** Climb easy rock up left in corners and grooves (4th class) to a big ledge. **Pitch 5:** Climb easy cracks and then a nice clean slab (5.5) to a small belay ledge. **Pitch 6:** Cruise a long right-facing corner and step left near its top to a good belay stance. **Pitch 7:** Best pitch. Climb a shallow left-facing corner (5.6) up the airy edge of the Northeast Face. At its top, move right and jam a nice crack (5.5) just left of a left-facing corner to a small stance on the exposed edge. **Pitch 8:** Step right and wrestle up a slot (5.6), then climb a crack (5.4) in the back of a chimney. End on a big belay ledge on the ridge. **Pitch 9:** Easy scrambling (3rd and 4th class) leads 200 feet to a ledge system on the west side of the summit. Squeeze up a slot (5.6) in a large block to emerge onto the airy summit. **Rack:** Light rack with sets of Stoppers and cams to #3, 200-foot (60-meter) rope.

Nan Darkus edging up the *South Face* route on the Petit Grepon.

PHOTO TOPHER DONAHUE

3.

Petit Grepon

Loch Vale, one of Rocky Mountain National Park's most scenic spots, descends northeast from the Continental Divide, dropping past alpine tarns and dense evergreen forests. Icy Brook, originating from Taylor Glacier, traverses the valley floor, tumbling over cliffs and twisting through meadows. The upper valley is lined on the north by the Cathedral Spires, a collection of rocky summits and faces including Cathedral Wall and farther west, a bunch of spires—Sharkstooth, Petit Grepon, The Saber, and The Foil.

The Petit Grepon is the most beautiful of these spires. This amazing semidetached pinnacle, flanked by Sharkstooth and The Saber, offers an 800-foot-high South Face that culminates with an airy postage-stamp summit, a flat rectangle 10 feet wide and 25 feet long.

The Petit Grepon's concave South Face offers two great routes that wander up cracks, chimneys, slabs, and headwalls to a couple of final pitches up a dramatic and exposed granite blade. The *South Face* route, one of Colorado's best alpine rock climbs, is very popular and can be crowded on summer weekends. The granite is excellent with incut holds and lots of cracks, and the climbing is varied, fun, exposed, and well protected. The *South Face* is one of Rocky Mountain's most popular alpine climbs, so unless you want to climb below other parties, risking rockfall and slowness, avoid weekends.

The climbing season runs from June through September. Snow generally melts off the south-facing wall by early June. Snowfields may be found on the approach hike, particularly on the steep trail section below Glass Lake and on the scree slope below the Petit Grepon. Be careful early in the season on the descent into The Gash on the backside. Snow and ice remain in the steep couloir well into summer.

The two routes are done as day climbs from Bear Lake Road. A limited number of bivouac sites are available for overnight stays. A bivy permit is obtained at the Backcountry Office, next to the Beaver Meadows Visitor Center. Watch for objective dangers that include rockfall from parties above, wet rock, loose blocks, afternoon thunderstorms, lightning strikes, and overcrowding. July and August weekends are the busiest days. Schedule your climb on a weekday or

Native Americans were the park's first climbers. The Arapahos captured eagles from a skin-covered trap atop Longs Peak, while lofty Trail Ridge was traversed by a 15-mile-long Ute trail called *Taieonbaa,* or "Child's Trail," which was used by early paleo-hunters beginning 12,000 years ago. Ancient Clovis points found atop the ridge testify to their early passage.

in September to avoid the rush or alter your plans and climb Sharkstooth or The Saber. A predawn start is essential to approach and climb the route before the usual afternoon storms.

Getting there: See map on page 28. Park at the small Glacier Gorge Trailhead on Bear Lake Road a mile from the road's end at Bear Lake (GPS: N 40.310491 / W -105.640419). The small lot fills up early, so no parking spaces may be available. Alternatively, park at the larger Bear Lake lot and hike 0.5 mile down to the Glacier Gorge Trailhead, or take the free shuttle from the Park & Ride lot across from Glacier Basin Campground. It's 4.6 miles from the trailhead to Sky Pond below the Petit Grepon and another 0.25 mile up to the wall base. Hike south on Glacier Gorge Trail for 1.4 miles to its junction with North Longs Peak Trail. Keep right and continue another 0.5 mile to the

junction of the Glacier Gorge and Loch Vale Trails. Keep right on Loch Vale Trail. The trail follows the valley for another 2.7 miles to Sky Pond at 10,900 feet, passing The Loch, a large lake. Just before Sky Pond, look for a climber's trail cutting right toward the talus slopes below The Saber and Petit Grepon. Scramble up talus to the base. Allow two hours to hike to the spire.

Descent: If you bivouac at the base, carry all your gear up the climb. If anything is left at the base, the best descent is to scramble up to the notch above The Gash, scramble east (3rd class) across the north side of The Saber to another notch, and descend south down a steep but easy gully to Sky Pond. A short rappel over a step from bolts is necessary partway down the gully. Avoid rappelling and downclimbing the steep gullies on either side of the Petit. While they look benign, most parties that do this descent end up with major problems because of loose rubble and stuck rappel ropes.

The descent is straightforward, but a wrong turn can turn it into an unexpected epic. Make a long two-rope rappel or three single-rope rappels into the steep gully on the northeast side of the tower from fixed summit anchors. From the base of the rappels, scramble up the gully and locate an easy fifth-class chimney. Climb the chimney and scramble up the gully to the East Col, a notch behind the Petit Grepon and between Sharkstooth and The Saber. Descend north down gullies and slabs into The Gash, a steep couloir that angles northeast. Descend this to Andrews Glacier Trail, which leads to Loch Vale.

Alternatively, make six rappels down the South Face with double 200-foot (60-meter) ropes. All rappels are from bolted stations. **First rappel:** Rappel 165 feet from the summit to a 2-bolt anchor. **Second rappel:** Rappel 135 feet to a 2-bolt anchor. **Third rappel:** Rappel 100 feet to a ledge. Scramble left and locate slings on a block below the ledge. Downclimb a chimney to the slings. **Fourth rappel:** Rappel 165 feet to the second terrace. **Fifth rappel:** Locate another set of bolts and rappel 200 feet to the first terrace. The next anchors are 50 feet right. **Sixth rappel:** Rappel 165 feet from a 2-bolt anchor on a boulder to the base.

1. South Face (III 5.8) The route follows an obvious crack system up the middle of the face to the right ridge, which leads to the summit. If the route is crowded, an easy alternative climbs just outside of and on the southeast ridge to the Pizza Pan Belay, six pitches up. Begin left of the main chimney. Scramble up right onto a ledge 70 feet above the base. **Pitches 1 and 2:** Climb the face left of the chimney (5.6) for 200 feet to a 30-foot-wide ledge called First Terrace. Climb in one pitch with a long rope. **Pitch 3:** Climb a chimney to a large chockstone. Pass it on the left and belay atop it. **Pitch 4:** Climb the left wall of the chimney

Petit Grepon—South Face

to a roof that caps it. Step out of the chimney into an awkward left-leaning crack (5.7) and follow it to the wide Second Terrace. **Pitch 5:** Bridge up the obvious chimney (5.5) above the ledge. Exit left atop the chimney, then work back right with face moves (5.6) to a belay stance. **Pitch 6:** Crux. Begin by climbing up right on a steep slab (5.7) to a good ledge. Stem, jam, and face climb a thin crack in a right-facing dihedral (5.8) to a ledge on the right-hand ridge. This long pitch is technical, exposed, and sustained. **Pitch 7:** Long, sustained, and scant pro. Climb a steep face (5.7) 30 feet right of the southeast ridge (right of the South Face). Higher, climb up left to Pizza Pan Belay, a tiny, exposed stance on the southeast corner below a jutting prow. **Pitch 8:** Climb a thin crack (5.7) above the belay to the face to the right. Continue up the vertical face to a ledge. Serious pitch—long, sustained, under-protected, and requires careful route-finding. **Pitch 9:** Fire straight up the headwall above on big holds (5.6) to the summit. **Rack:** Sets of Stoppers, TCUs, and Friends or Camalots to 3 inches; extra 2-foot runners; two 200-foot (60-meter) ropes.

2. Southwest Corner (III 5.9) Joins the *South Face* at the Pizza Pan Belay and finishes up its last two pitches. The route follows a crack system left of the regular route to the Second Terrace, before climbing up left onto the southwest corner. The upper section is sustained and exposed. Begin by picking a crack line on the slabs left of the main lower chimney. **Pitch 1:** Climb easy cracks and slabs for a full rope-length to the First Terrace. **Pitch 2:** Follow an arching left-facing dihedral (5.5) to a belay stance above the arch. **Pitch 3:** Climb the dihedral (bit of 5.6) to the Second Terrace. Go left on the ledge 50 feet to start the next lead. **Pitch 4:** Climb shallow corners, cracks, and steep slabs (5.7) up left to a ledge just left of the southwest corner. **Pitch 5:** Work up corners and cracks (5.8) on the sharp ridge for a long, sustained pitch. Belay at the second ledge on the exposed ridge. **Pitch 6:** Climb the arête to a vertical crack (5.9). Belay above on a ledge directly below the narrow prow of the South Face. **Pitch 7:** Make a short traverse right across the face to the Pizza Pan Belay on the southeast ridge. This short lead can be combined with pitch 6, but use slings for rope drag. **Pitch 8:** Finish up *South Face*. Climb a crack/flake (5.7) above the belay and work up right on exposed face climbing to a ledge. **Pitch 9:** Finish up steep rock (5.6) to the ridge above. Climb direct to the summit. **Rack:** Sets of Stoppers, TCUs, and Friends or Camalots to 3 inches; extra 2-foot runners; two 200-foot (60-meter) ropes.

4.

Hallett Peak

The steep northeast face of 12,713-foot-high Hallett Peak towers west of Bear Lake, forming one of Rocky Mountain National Park's most beautiful mountain vistas. The face's three buttresses, composed of metamorphic schist and gneiss and chiseled by the Tyndall Glacier, offer excellent multi-pitch alpine climbing adventures.

Hallett Peak's best climbing is found on the 900-foot-high Second Buttress in the middle. The dark cleft of Hallett Chimney separates it from the First Buttress on the left, while the Third Buttress is to its right. The Second Buttress offers excellent climbing on mostly clean rock split by thin cracks and corners and rippled with finger-friendly edges. The routes are long and sometimes runout on the easier sections. Successful ascents require an early start to avoid thunderstorms, good route-finding skills, and the ability to find gear placements.

The compact rock on the Second Buttress offers lots of edges, flakes, and incut handholds, allowing competent climbers to move almost anywhere on the face. Crack systems tend to be intermittent, so routes wander around and connect various features. Eyeball your proposed route from the lake below before setting off and memorize features to keep you on course.

The best season is June to mid-September. The northeast-facing Second Buttress receives sun in the morning but falls into shadow by midday. Thunderstorms, rolling in from the west, are unseen until they're on you. Start early to avoid rain and lightning. Watch for rockfall from parties above and wear a helmet. Lots of loose rock is found on this high alpine wall.

Getting there: See map on page 28. Find Hallett Peak by driving up Bear Lake Road from the Beaver Meadows Entrance to a parking lot at the road's end by Bear Lake (GPS: N 40.311910 / -W 105.645480). This lot is usually busy, especially in summer. Get there early to grab a parking spot or take the free shuttle from the Glacier Basin Park & Ride lot to Bear Lake. The trail approach to the face is about 2 miles; allow one to one-and-a-half hours of uphill hiking from Bear Lake to the cliff. From the 9,420-foot Bear Lake trailhead, walk south from the lake to Emerald Lake Trail. Follow it west up Tyndall Gorge. The trail passes Nymph Lake (0.5 mile) and Dream Lake (1.1 miles), and reaches 10,080-foot Emerald Lake after 1.8 miles (GPS: N 40.309602 / W -105.666593). Find a path that climbs onto a terrace above the lake's south shore. Boulder-hop across it and then hike up talus slopes to the cliff base. Snowfields are found below the wall until late July.

Descent: The descent off Hallett Peak is complicated. The best descent is to hike west from the top of the face across the summit plateau. A steep gully borders the west edge of the Third Buttress. Scramble down the loose gully for a few hundred feet to a fork. Scramble up to a notch on the left to avoid cliffs at the gully's bottom. From the notch, descend another gully to the wall's base. Use caution if other climbers are below, and watch for steep snow in the gully.

An alternative descent goes south from the First Buttress to a headwall with bolted rappel anchors. From the cliff top, scramble east along the ridge crest past the First Buttress to bolt anchors. Make two single-line rappels into a gully. Scramble northeast down the gully for a few hundred feet, then climb up left (3rd class) and then down another gully to the base of Hallett Chimney.

1. Love Route (III 5.9 or 5.7 A1) One of Hallett's best moderates. This route follows the right side of a triangular buttress before weaving up the wall left of an arching crack system. The first two pitches are long or can break into three pitches; the last two pitches can also break into three. Begin right of the triangular-shaped buttress. **Pitches 1 and 2:** Climb a right-facing dihedral (5.3–5.6) up the right side of the buttress. Watch for loose rock. **Pitch 3:** Leave the dihedral and climb the blocky buttress face (easy 5th class) to its top. Continue above the buttress to a belay ledge atop a flake. **Pitch 4:** Face climb a steep wall past incipient cracks (5.6) for 130 feet to a small stance. Aim for a dark roof near the top of the Second Buttress. **Pitch 5:** Superb face climbing (5.7) up the wall to a sloping belay ramp below the roof. Expect sustained climbing. **Pitch 6:** Crux lead. Climb to a dark left-facing dihedral on the right side of the roof. Climb the steep dihedral (5.9) past fixed pitons. Aid by pulling on pitons. Angle left above the roof up a shallow groove. Climb easily to the top. **Rack:** Large RPs, set of Stoppers with extra small sizes, set of Camalots to #3, 200-foot (60-meter) rope.

2. Hesse-Ferguson (III 5.9 R) Excellent granite, superb face climbing, exposure, and good pro—a classic alpine climb. Ascends the shield of

The Third Buttress of Hallett Peak fell on July 28, 1956, to Ray Northcutt and Harvey T. Carter, two of Colorado's best climbers in the 1950s. The pair talked up their shady route—*Northcutt-Carter*—as being one of America's most difficult rock climbs. The rumor was dispelled in 1959 after the second ascent party, Californians Yvon Chouinard and Ken Weeks, strolled up the reportedly formidable route in a mere four hours in the late afternoon . . . so much for Colorado's hardest big wall!

rock between the arching crack of *Englishman's Route* and the nose of the Second Buttress on the right. A right-hand variation on pitches 3 and 4 makes this one of Hallett's best climbs. Variations exist on every pitch. Begin by locating the huge, right-facing dihedral on the broken buttress ascended by the *Love Route*. *Hesse-Ferguson* starts 100 feet right of the big dihedral on a ledge below a left-leaning, right-facing corner. Scramble to the ledge and belay. **Pitch 1:** Climb a left-angling, right-facing corner (5.5) for a long pitch to a belay stance. **Pitch 2:** Continue up the corner system (5.7) to a ledge below some white roofs. **Pitch 3:** Two variations start here. Each is two pitches, which can be combined with a long rope. **Variation A:** Traverse right and climb a right-facing corner (5.8) to a roof. Pass it on the left and edge up right on thin face moves (5.9 R) to a belay stance below a shallow right-facing corner. **Variation A Pitch 4:** Climb a right-facing dihedral (5.9) and climb up left to a terrace. **Variation B:** Follow the *Love Route* (5.7), then work up right past a small roof and across a slab to a belay stance below a roof. **Variation B Pitch 4:** Climb a right-facing corner (5.7), pull over a roof (5.9), and cruise (5.7 R) to the terrace. **Pitch 5:** Climb a right-facing corner (5.7) to a small roof. Move right and climb up left (5.7 R) to a belay at a flake. **Pitch 6:** Face climb up right (5.7) to a thin crack. Face climb straight up along the crack then over the right

side of a roof (5.8) and belay above in a white rock band. **Pitch 7:** Climb a narrow corner (5.8) to some roofs. Traverse right (5.8) and belay in a groove. **Pitch 8:** Finish up *Culp-Bossier*. Crimp small edges (5.8) on the face right of a right-facing dihedral. Pass a roof and climb easily to the top. **Rack:** Set of Stoppers with extra medium sizes, RPs, TCUs, set of cams to 3 inches, 200-foot (60-meter) rope.

3. Culp-Bossier (III 5.8+) Excellent classic route with moderate climbing and exposure on the nose of the Second Buttress. The climbing is straightforward, although a few sections have problematic route-finding. Expect runouts on the easier climbing. Start from the same ledge below a left-leaning, right-facing corner as *Hesse-Ferguson*. **Pitch 1:** Climb the corner for 50 feet before striking out right onto the face. Climb a fun finger crack (5.7) up right to a belay stance. 140 feet. **Pitch 2:** Climb past a small roof and then head up left (5.6) to a right-facing dihedral. This is the middle of three right-facing dihedrals. Belay atop the corner. **Pitch 3:** Traverse right on a ramp (5.8), reach past a small roof, and climb a right-leaning corner (5.7). Finish by face climbing up left to a terrace in a band of white rock. Share this belay ledge with *Hesse-Ferguson*. **Pitch 4:** Begin on the ledge's right side. Face climb up the left edge of a sweeping prow. Belay on a small stance. This long pitch is slightly under-protected, but stays at 5.6 if you find the right line. **Pitch 5:** Continue up the prow (5.8) using edges on exposed rock. Near the top of the nose, keep left and avoid a ramp that swings up right. Instead, climb up left to a belay below a groove/crack. **Pitch 6:** Climb a groove (5.8) with jams and stems to a belay ledge. **Pitch 7:** Face climb (5.8) up a wall right of an obvious right-facing dihedral, avoiding overhangs. The angle and difficulty ease below the summit. **Rack:** RPs; sets of Stoppers, TCUs, and cams to 3 inches.

4. Jackson-Johnson (III 5.9 or 5.7 A1) Popular moderate up the right side of the Second Buttress. It follows the left side of a pillar before striking up a steep headwall to the sloping summit. The 5.9 climbing is out of character with the rest of the route; many climbers grab gear on it. Begin right of a right-facing dihedral below the same leaning corner as *Culp-Bossier*. **Pitch 1:** Climb light rock (5.6) and then a left-leaning, right-facing dihedral to a small ledge. Traverse right from the ledge to a short headwall split by a finger crack (5.7). Belay atop a flake. 145 feet. **Pitch 2:** Climb a steep, awkward crack past an overhang (5.5), then angle up right across slabs to a belay in a right-facing corner. 125 feet. **Pitch 3:** Traverse up right across an easy slab (5.4), climb a groove, and continue to a belay below a chimney. **Pitch 4:** Climb the easy chimney before heading up right to the left side of a pillar.

Follow the chimney/crack system (initially 5.6) up the pillar to a convenient belay stance. **Pitch 5:** Continue up the easy chimney to a spacious belay ledge atop the pillar. Pitches 4 and 5 can be combined. **Pitch 6:** Angle up left through a couple of right-facing corners (5.6) to a ledge on the left below a right-leaning, right-facing dihedral. Watch for rope drag or split the pitch into two short leads. **Pitch 7:** Crux. Stem, jam, and thrutch up an awkward right-facing dihedral past old bolts and fixed pitons (5.9 or A0). Work left around a corner from the top of the dihedral to a belay stance. **Pitch 8:** Short, easy lead up loose blocks and boulders to the top. **Rack:** Sets of Stoppers, TCUs, and Camalots to #3.

Layton Kor climbed Hallett Peak lots of times in the 1960s, including the second ascent of *Jackson-Johnson*, as well as his own first ascents. "I've been in some really bad rain and hail storms on Halletts," Layton said. "It always hits when you're three-quarters of the way up the wall. Three times I was in really bad lightning storms at the top. It's all kinda flat up there. It's a dangerous place. One time my hair was crackling and all my pitons were buzzing. We didn't know much about lightning back then. We should have laid down. We could have been killed."

Caroline George on the *Culp-Bossier* route on Hallett Peak. PHOTO TOPHER DONAHUE

Lumpy Ridge

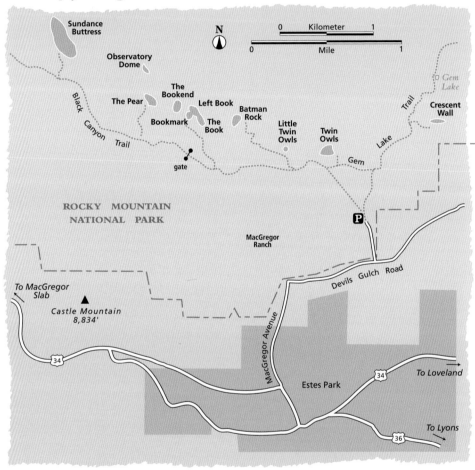

Sundance Buttress

Observatory Dome

N

0   Kilometer   1

0   Mile   1

The Bookend

The Pear

Left Book

Batman Rock

Black Canyon Trail

Bookmark

The Book

Little Twin Owls

Twin Owls

Lake Trail

To Gem Lake

Crescent Wall

Gem

gate

ROCKY MOUNTAIN NATIONAL PARK

P

MacGregor Ranch

Devils Gulch Road

To MacGregor Slab

Castle Mountain 8,834'

MacGregor Avenue

34

34

To Loveland

Estes Park

36

To Lyons

5.

Lumpy Ridge

Lumpy Ridge, lying in the northeastern sector of Rocky Mountain National Park and north of Estes Park, offers a sunny climbing playground with over thirty-five named crags on its 3-mile-long south-facing ridge. Its scattered lumps of granite form the park's most popular climbing area, providing a huge variety of great climbs on perfect stone. Most routes are climbed in a traditional style, requiring the placement and removal of gear. A few bolted climbs are found, but are the exception.

A compact crystal-studded granite forms Lumpy's cliffs. The slabby cliffs repose at a 70-degree angle, allowing climbers to use small features, edges, and smears on rock that appears to be featureless at first glance. Lumpy's cliffs, untouched by the glaciers that once blanketed the rest of the park's peaks, were gently shaped by water and freeze-and-thaw cycles that formed exfoliation slabs, flakes, vertical cracks and chimneys, and potholes.

Over 500 routes ascend Lumpy's crags. Most are climbed traditionally, with the leader placing protection and setting up belays. Few sport climbs are found. Fixed protection is rare on most Lumpy climbs. Bring a standard climbing rack with sets of wired nuts, TCUs,

cams up to 4 inches, and a fistful of slings. Some routes require small brass nuts or wide crack gear like Big Bros or #5 Camalots. Hexentric nuts also work well in Lumpy's flared cracks. A 165-foot (50-meter) rope is still standard at Lumpy, although longer cords allow you to combine pitches. Due to heavy use, human waste disposal bags are strongly encouraged.

Getting there: Lumpy Ridge is easily accessed from Boulder, Denver, and Fort Collins. Estes Park is 30 miles west of Loveland and 34 miles west of I-25 via US 34. From Boulder and Denver, drive north from Boulder on US 36 to Lyons. Continue 19 miles west on US 36 to Estes Park. From the east side of Estes Park, drive north on MacGregor Avenue for a couple of miles to MacGregor Ranch. Here the road bends east and becomes Devils Gulch Road. Follow this road another mile to the Lumpy Ridge Trailhead parking on the left (north) side of the road (GPS: N 40.396437 / W -105.512818). This is the trailhead for Gem Lake, Twin Owls, and Black Canyon Trails. The parking area fills up on weekends.

Follow Gem Lake Trail to Crescent Wall, Twin Owls Trail to the Twin Owls, and Black Canyon Trail to the rest of the crags.

Quinn Brett works across the crux traverse of *Finger Lickin' Good* on the Crescent Wall at Lumpy Ridge.

Rocky Mountain National Park offers excellent habitat for raptors, including eagles and falcons. Every year parts of the park are closed to climbing so nesting birds are undisturbed. These closures, from March through July, are usually at Lumpy Ridge and include Twin Owls, Batman Rock, Batman Pinnacle, and other cliffs. Closures also extend 100 yards in all directions from the rock formations and include descent routes and access trails. Check trailhead kiosks and www.nps.gov/romo for closure information.

CRESCENT WALL

The south-facing Crescent Wall is a slab with a crescent-shaped arch at Lumpy's east end. The wall offers some excellent crack routes along with good friction climbing on steep slabs. The difficulty of most routes limits its popularity, so it's rare to find other climbers here. The wall is hot in summer, making it ideal during cooler months.

Finding the cliff: Hike northeast on Gem Lake Trail from the Lumpy Ridge Trailhead parking area (GPS: N 40.396437 / W -105.512818). Follow the trail for about 1.5 miles until it bends north above a shallow, boulder-choked ravine. Crescent Wall is visible directly east. Follow a climber's trail into the ravine and scramble over boulders to the cliff base (GPS: N 40.406112 / W -105.504212).

Descent: Descend off the wall by hiking west down ramps and ledges.

Watching wildlife is a popular Rocky Mountain National Park activity. Most folks come to glimpse the big critters—elk, bighorn sheep, mule, deer, and moose. In all, almost 65 species of mammals, 281 species of birds, 11 fish, 6 amphibians, and 1 reptile inhabit the park. Some of the best places to see animals are Trail Ridge Road, Moraine Park, and Horseshoe Park. Always watch from a distance—your presence stresses the animals. Don't get too close—large animals are dangerous. And don't feed panhandling squirrels and deer.

Crescent Wall

1. Finger Lickin' Good (5.11a) Excellent finger crack. **Pitch 1:** Climb along a thin crack that diagonals up right. The first 20 feet of face climbing is the hardest section (5.11a). Belay from gear at a stance below a finger crack. **Pitch 2:** Jam the finger crack for 50 feet to a 2-bolt anchor atop a flake. **Rack:** Double sets of Stoppers and TCUs, small cams.

2. Pressure Drop (5.11a) More great jamming! Begin left of a small arch. Jam a splitter hand and finger crack (5.10d) to a fixed piton. Sustained face moves lead up right along an angling seam to a second crux (5.10d). From a flake, hand traverse (tricky gear) right to *Finger Lickin' Good*'s 2-bolt anchor.

Descent: Rappel 80 feet. **Rack:** Sets of RPs, Stoppers with extra small and medium sizes, and TCUs; cams to #.75 Camalot.

3. Milk Run (5.7 R) Begin at the far left side. **Pitch 1:** Climb a shallow right-facing corner (5.6) to a belay ledge with a small tree. **Pitch 2:** Friction up right on an unprotected slab.

4. Friction Addition (5.11d) Start at a tree. Crimp past a bolt to an overlap. Hard moves (5.11d) lead to the next bolt. Finish up easier but runout rock to a belay. 5 bolts. Finish up *Heaven Can Wait*. **Rack:** #0 and #1 TCUs, quickdraws, and a long sling.

TWIN OWLS

The aptly named Twin Owls roost on the ridge northwest of the parking area. The 300 foot-high, overhanging south face hosts some of Lumpy's hardest crack climbs, including a couple of strenuous off-width cracks. The *Central Chimney* splits the south face, separating the two owls. The Roosting Ramp sweeps up left and allows access to routes on the west Owl. A lower broken buttress sits below the Owls, while the Hen and Chickens are below the crag's southeast corner. The crag may be closed from spring to midsummer for nesting raptors. Check the kiosk board at the parking area for closure information.

Finding the cliff: From the Lumpy Ridge Trailhead parking lot on Devils Gulch Road (GPS: N40.396437 / W -105.512818), hike 0.5 mile west to the Twin Owls Trail and follow it to the Owls. The marked climber's access trail begins 0.25 mile up the main trail. Turn north and follow it to the base of the Roosting Ramp. Don't shortcut and cause erosion; use the trail.

Descent: The best descent from the summit is from the saddle between the two Owls. From the low point between the Owls, descend north down a Fourth-class gully on the backside. Locate a crack threaded with rappel slings under a boulder. Make a 75-foot rappel to the base. An alternative is to downclimb or rappel the *Bowels of the Owls* route.

After downclimbing the gully, find rap slings on a boulder above a rabbit hole. Downclimb a funky chimney (5.0) or rappel 70 feet. Can be wet, slimy, or icy. Scope out the descent before starting to avoid problems.

In the 1980s British solo climber Derek Hersey, living in Boulder, made an audacious free-solo ascent of The Crack of Fear on Twin Owls. Crusher Bartlett, one of his roommates, says, "Derek never really talked about it much—it was not one of his better moments." Derek hitchhiked up to Estes Park and went up to on-sight solo the crack. He knew nothing about the climb, although he had seen it and figured since it was rated 5.10+ that he would cruise it. He set off and soon found it much harder than he imagined. "Committed, and realizing his mistake too late," says Crusher, "he had to fight for his life. His knee was ripped up badly, and he could not climb for a while afterward. In fact, he could barely walk. He was limping badly for some time. Hitchhiking back, with his knee ripped up and blood all over, must have been interesting."

Vera Schulte-Pelkum leads *Crack of Fear*, Lumpy Ridge's off-width testpiece.

PHOTO TOPHER DONAHUE

1. East Ridge (5.8) Fine climb on the east edge of the Owls. Start from a flake at the southeast corner behind the Hen and Chickens formation. **Pitch 1:** Climb the left crack, then exit left (5.8) at a small roof. Continue up a couple of flake cracks (mild 5.8 cruxes) to easier terrain. Belay on a ledge, then move the belay up right. **Pitch 2:** Climb over a block to an A-shaped roof. Pull out the right side (5.7) and face climb (5.7 R) to a ledge or tackle a crack direct over the roof (5.8). From the ledge, climb easy rock (5.4) to the summit. **Rack:** Sets of Stoppers, TCUs, and Camalots to #3.

2. Twister (5.10b) Full-body experience! Follows a chimney in a left-facing dihedral on the right side. Begin by scrambling 50 feet and belaying below the dihedral. **Pitch 1:** Climb a slot to an awkward mantle. Work up the easier chimney until it pinches down, then grapple up a short section of body jams in the tight chimney (5.10b). Work up the moderate chimney to a belay on a narrow shelf to the left. 80 feet. **Pitch 2:** Continue up the chimney past a chockstone (5.9) for 50 feet. Finish up the wider chimney to a ledge. 65 feet. **Pitch 3:** Climb cracks to a horizontal crack topped by a roof. Step left and jam a sharp fist crack (5.9) over a bulge to the summit. 130 feet. **Rack:** Sets of Stoppers and TCUs; Camalots to #2 and two #3 Camalots, one #4, and two #5.

3. Crack of Fear (5.10d) Strenuous, sustained, and unrelenting—Colorado's most famous off-width crack. Crack is 5 inches or wider for 250 feet. It's safely climbed with big cams and Big Bros. Many climbers rap from 75 feet before the route crux. To start, find a long off-width crack right of the *Central Chimney.* **Pitch 1:** Jam the left side (5.9) of the Rat's Tooth, a pillar below the crack. Work up the off-width crack (5.9), right side in, to face moves. End at a shelf with bolt anchors on the left. 80 feet. If you have trouble here—bail now! **Pitch 2:** Struggle up the awkward 10-inch crack (5.10d) until it doglegs left. Undercling up left (5.10c) and climb to a belay stance. 70 feet. **Pitch 3:** Continue up the off-width crack (5.9 and 5.10) to a belay or stretch the rope to the top. **Pitch 4:** Climb up left from a horizontal break to the summit. **Rack:** Wide gear—everything you own. Double Camalots from #4 to #5 plus Big Bros.

4. Central Chimney (5.8) A spelunking adventure. Start below the deep chimney separating the Owls. **Pitch 1:** Climb the right side of a pedestal in the chimney, then head up left to a flake belay. **Pitch 2:** Continue up a squeeze chimney (5.7+) to a large chockstone. Turn it on the left and belay in an alcove. **Pitch 3:** Head up the chimney to a funky roof (5.7) or face climb (5.7) up the left wall. **Pitch 4:** Wander up the wall to the saddle between the Owls.

5. Tiger's Tooth (5.10-) Excellent climb on the right side of a detached pillar on the southwest corner. Begin from the Roosting Ramp below an off-width crack. **Pitch 1:** Fist jams and off-width moves (5.9+) grunt up the strenuous crack for 60 feet to an easier squeeze chimney (5.8). Look for hidden holds. Belay on the pillar. **Pitch 2:** Step onto the main face and follow a flared groove (5.7) and then easier rock to the top. Or step right and climb a thin crack (5.9). **Rack:** Stoppers and small cams, Camalots from #3 to #5, #3 Big Bro.

6. Wolf's Tooth (5.9-) Superb, strenuous, and sustained. Climbs the west side of the *Tiger's Tooth* pillar. Jam *Conads* for a great starting pitch. **Pitch 1:** Jam a hand and fist crack (5.9-) that widens into a chimney after 45 feet. Work up the chimney (5.8) to a belay below the pillar's top. **Pitch 2:** Step onto the main face and follow a flared groove (5.7) and then easier rock to the top. Or step right and climb a thin crack (5.9). **Rack:** Stoppers and small cams, Camalots to #4 and a #4.5 or #5.

7. Conads (5.9) Good jamming on the Lower Owls. Preferred start to *Wolf's Tooth*. Start below a hand crack on the west side. Stem up a slot to a block roof and jam past it on the right (5.8). Throw hand jams up the steep splitter (5.9) to an easier finish (5.5). **Rack:** Camalots to #3 with extra hand-sizes.

8. Tilted Mitten (5.8) On the Lower Owls. Begin at the lowest point of the south face. **Pitch 1:** Climb either of two low-angle chimneys that head up right to a good ledge. **Pitch 2:** Climb an arching crack to the bottom of The Mitten formation. Jam The Mitten's right side (5.8) to a hole that leads to a ledge. **Pitch 3:** Work right up a chimney and cracks to the Roosting Ramp.

9. Prow (5.10c) Fun route up the prow of the Lower Owls. Start by climbing the first two pitches of *Tilted Mitten*. Belay on the left side of a ledge. Work left to a prow and jam a crack over a roof (5.10c). Continue up easier rock to the Roosting Ramp.

LITTLE TWIN OWLS

Little Twin Owls, a small trailside crag west of the Twin Owls, resembles the big Owls on the ridge above. It offers a couple of climbs that are easily accessed for a quick pump. A prominent wide crack divides the two rounded summits.

Anaconda (5.13b/c), Lumpy Ridge's hardest crack climb, jams a fingertip crack up an overhanging wall on the south face of the West Twin Owl. This spectacular line was first aided by Layton Kor and Larry Dalke in 1965. In 1993, Boulder crackmaster Alan Lester jammed the first crack on top-rope, then led it the following year with a few fixed pieces of gear. Later Tommy Caldwell led it without preplaced gear and in 2005, Beth Rodden made the third ascent.

Finding the cliff: From the Lumpy Ridge Trailhead parking lot (GPS: N 40.396437 / W -105.512818), hike west to Black Canyon Trail. Past the Twin Owls, look for a junction (GPS: N 40.401540 / W -105.522005) and go right on the higher of two trails toward Batman Rock. The obvious formation is on the right just past the junction (GPS: N 40.402642 / W -105.523936).

1. Little Twin Owls Finger Crack

(5.11a) Usually toproped. Start below a finger crack on the south side of the south Little Owl. Jam and layback the strenuous crack to a 2-bolt anchor. To access the anchors: Climb an easy route (5.0) up the west side to the north Little Owl, then step across the gap to the summit anchors. **Rack:** A couple of sets of Stoppers, TCUs, and small to medium cams.

2. Southeast Arête

(5.11c) Toprope. Crimp up the right side of the rounded arête right of the finger crack.

Little Twin Owls

BATMAN ROCK

Batman Rock sits high atop the ridge west of the Twin Owls. Knobby slabs, intermittent crack systems, and long overlaps characterize the dome. A blunt prow divides Batman's East and South Faces. All the described routes are on the East Face.

Finding the dome: From the Lumpy Ridge Trailhead parking area on Devils Gulch Road (GPS: N 40.396437 / W -105.512818), hike west 0.7 mile to Black Canyon Trail. Pass beneath the Little Twin Owls. At an obvious trail junction, go right on a good trail to Batman Rock. At a second Y-junction, go left to Checkerboard Rock and then up to Batman Pinnacle.

Descent: To descend from the summit, scramble north on slabs to a gully that leads back to the base of the East Face.

1. Bat Crack (5.9 R) Classic climb. Start below a crack in the middle of the East Face and 30 feet left of a crack with a tree. **Pitch 1:** Face climb (5.8) directly up to the crack or climb easier rock to the left. Climb the crack and then face climb up left (5.8 R) to a short crack. Finish up easier rock (5.6 R) to a hanging belay below a notch in the big overlap. 140 feet. **Pitch 2:** Layback over the double roof above (5.9). Jam a finger crack to the summit. **Rack:** Sets of TCUs and Stoppers, RPs, small to medium cams.

Batman Rock

2. Hand Over Hand (5.7) Fun climbing. Combine pitches with a 70-meter cord. Start 35 feet left of *Bat Crack* inside a chimney that separates the main face from a block. **Pitch 1:** Grab knobs up a face (5.5) for 25 feet, then jam a hand crack behind a flake right of a left-facing dihedral *(Marlin Alley)* to a possible belay under a roof. Make an exciting hand traverse up left for 30 feet to a break in the roof. Pull over the roof (5.7) and climb to a belay ledge. **Pitch 2:** Two finishes. Climb up left on easier rock (5.6) to the summit or climb up right and then back left along the edge of a left-facing corner (5.8). **Rack:** Sets of Stoppers, TCUs, and cams to 3 inches.

3. Marlin Alley (5.11b) Excellent and pumpy. Same start as *Hand Over Hand*. Climb an unprotected knobby face (5.5) for 25 feet and move up left along an angling flake, which becomes a left-facing corner. Climb the corner, which steepens when you reach a hand crack on the right wall. Jam the hands to off-fingers crack

(5.10c) or continue up the corner (5.10a) to a big roof. Crank the right side of the roof (5.11b) with jams and sidepulls to jugs above and a mantle (5.9). Continue past the next overlap (5.9) and scamper to the summit. Use lots of slings for rope drag or belay at *Hand Over Hand*'s belay. **Rack:** Sets of Stoppers and cams to 3 inches with doubles between 2 and 3 inches, lots of slings, 200-foot (60-meter) rope.

4. Clowntime Is Over (5.9) Good and popular. Belay atop a detached block above the start of *Hand Over Hand*. **Pitch 1:** Fall across a gap and grab a flake (scary 5.7). Face climb up left on a slab (5.6) to a belay atop a flake on a prow. **Pitch 2:** Edge directly up the prow to the left side of a big roof. Reach over the roof, grab a jug, and pull over (5.9). Climb over another roof (5.9) or pass it to the left (5.7) and climb to a sloping ledge. Belay here or climb easier rock (5.6) to the top. **Rack:** Sets of Stoppers, TCUs, and small to medium cams.

BATMAN PINNACLE

Batman Pinnacle, a tower with a south face, is below Batman Rock's South Face. The secluded crag offers one of Lumpy's best climbs up its 350-foot face. It's busy on weekends. After climbing, head up to Batman and crank one of its routes for the full-meal deal.

Finding the cliff: From the Lumpy Ridge Trailhead parking on Devils Gulch Road (GPS: N 40.396437 / W -105.512818), hike west 0.7 mile to Black Canyon Trail. Pass the Little Twin Owls. At a trail junction, go left (the right fork goes to Batman Rock). The trail is hard to follow at times. Alternatively, approach the pinnacle from Batman Rock by scrambling down the east side of the formation to the pinnacle's south face.

1. Batman and Robin (5.6) Great superheroes journey. Combine pitches with a long rope. Start by a couple of dead trees. **Pitch 1:** Either climb up right (5.5) to a belay at the base of a left-facing corner or start to the left and climb a face to a shallow corner (5.5) to the belay ledge. 65 feet. **Pitch 2:** Work up right and climb a right-facing dihedral (5.4) to a belay. **Pitch 3:** Three cracks are above. Jam the flared middle crack (5.6) or the right one (5.7) to an alcove below a small roof. Pass the roof on the left and cruise easy rock to a stance on the left edge of the summit block. **Pitch 4:** Climb a short corner (5.5) and finish up the left side of the block. **Descent:** Rappel 150 feet north from anchors. Scramble east down to a gully. Follow the gully back to the base by downclimbing or rappelling from trees. **Rack:** Sets of Stoppers and cams to 3 inches.

Lots of climbing accidents have occurred at Lumpy Ridge beginning with Stan Shepard's 50-foot fall on the Twin Owls when his aid pitons pulled on the overhanging South Wall in 1963. Stan broke his neck, was rescued, and recovered. Since Lumpy is a traditional climbing area, many accidents occur from falls onto improperly placed cams and nuts which pull out. Other accidents happen from rockfall, loose holds, rappel anchors and mishaps, and climbing beyond one's ability. The two Lumpy fatalities occurred from a fall on an unprotected slab and lightning on an approach trail. Wear a helmet and climb safely.

Batman Pinnacle

rappel 150'
off backside

route
hidden

Lightning
Rock

7

4

1

THE BOOK

The Book is Lumpy's best and most popular climbing sector. The south-facing cliff, reaching heights of 500 feet, offers classic routes up clean faces and cracks. The Book's compact granite is ideal for climbing adventures with incut edges, knobs, and crystals, allowing superb face moves and excellent friction smears. The cracks readily take pro so you can sew up most climbs.

A huge, left-facing dihedral divides The Book into two halves. The right side splits into two distinct sectors. The Pages Wall on the left is creased by vertical cracks, forming The Book's pages. The right side is the smooth J-Crack Slab. The best climbs described here ascend these two sectors.

Finding the cliff: From the Lumpy Ridge Trailhead parking area on Devils Gulch Road (GPS: N 40.396437 / W -105.512818), hike west 0.7 mile to Black Canyon Trail. Continue for a mile until you're south of The Book. The Book access trail heads northwest and climbs a steep slope to the cliff base below J-Crack Slab. Routes are described from right to left when facing the cliff.

Descent: Descend from the summit by scrambling southeast down slabs and gullies around the cliff's east flank.

1. Femp (5.9) Beautiful climb up a striking hand crack on the slab's right side. Start left of a gully groove. **Pitch 1:** Climb corners and cracks (5.5) to a belay ledge below a crack or climb *The Cavity* 40 feet left. 75 feet. **Pitch 2:** Start off the ledge's right side. Jam a crack (5.9) until it jogs left to another crack. Jam this easier crack (5.7) and finish up a left-facing corner (5.9) to a sloping stance. Use a 200-foot (60-meter) rope. **Pitch 3:** Various happy endings. *Right Exit,* the original finish, follows a left-leaning corner capped by a roof (5.7), then angles up right through a break in the upper roofs (5.7) to easier rock. Better to climb the last pitch of *Endless Crack.* Climb up right and jam a thin left-angling crack (5.9) to a break in the upper roofs. Pull over the roof with a wedged flake (5.9+) and cruise. **Rack:** Sets of Stoppers, TCUs, and cams to 3 inches with extra medium sizes; 200-foot (60-meter) rope.

2. The Cavity (5.10a) Good start for *Femp* and *J-Crack.* Begin by scrambling into a crystal-filled cavity with a pine tree above the cliff base. Layback up a left-facing corner to a large ledge below J-Crack Slab. Continue up *Femp.*

3. Kite Slab (5.11d) This route, the third pitch of *Pizza Face,* is a good third lead for *Femp.* Work right from *Femp*'s second belay to the base of the slab. Edge up right past three bolts to a high belay. Traverse off right on easy rock.

4. J-Crack (5.11c or 5.10a) Lumpy's most famous climb follows a

The Book

backwards J-Crack that begins 100 feet off the ground on the left side. **Pitch 1:** Face climb (5.6) to a groove and follow it to a slot (5.7). End on *Femp's* belay ledge. Set your belay on the ledge's left side. Alternatively, climb *The Cavity*. **Pitch 2:** Face climb delicately up left (5.8) to the bottom of J-Crack. Jam the flared finger and thin hand crack (sustained 5.9) for 140 feet to a cramped belay below the upper headwall. **Pitch 3:** Several alternatives. **A)** The hardest line continues up the crack with good fingerlocks and bad feet on the steep 25-foot-high headwall (5.11c) to a ledge above. **B)** The popular line jams to the headwall and traverses right on unprotected face moves (5.10a R) to an easy slanting groove/crack that leads to a ledge above the crack. Place pro high in the crack for security on the traverse. **C)** The easiest line traverses left (5.9 R) to a crack (5.8) on *Visual Aids* that leads to an awkward belay. **Pitch 4:** From the belay atop the crack on the first two variations, the best finishing pitch angles up right over a roof (5.7), up a slab, and through a break in the roofs above (5.7). Or climb easy grooves up left and then right to The Cave, a wide chimney. From The Cave the best exit is *Hurley Traverse,* which hand traverses (5.8) out right along a crack to a knob and then climbs up left. **Rack:** Stoppers with extra medium sizes, TCUs, and small to medium Friends; RPs for the headwall.

5. Loose Ends (5.9) Excellent varied climbing. Start below a left-facing corner on a flake. **Pitch 1:** Fingerlock or layback a finger crack in the well-protected corner (5.9) to the top of a flake. Undercling left onto a ramp and climb (5.8) up left to a belay pocket. **Pitch 2:** Traverse 10 feet left to two vertical finger cracks. Jam the second one (insecure 5.9 then sustained 5.8) to a belay above a flake. **Pitch 3:** Climb a short face to a left-leaning, left-facing dihedral. Layback up the dihedral (5.9) to a ledge. **Pitch 4:** Move right across an easy slab and up a groove to The Cave. Belay or continue up The Cave via a slot left of a block. Finish easily to The Book's right skyline. **Rack:** Sets of Stoppers, TCUs, and cams from ½ inch to 4 inches with doubles from ½ inch to 2 inches.

6. Pear Buttress (5.8+) Classic Book crack. Begin left of *Loose Ends* below a face right of a right-facing corner on the right side of a flake. This is where the access trail ends. **Pitch 1:** Face climb up left (5.7 R) to a stance 20 feet up. Step right into a crack and follow it to the flake's top. Make a hard move into twin cracks (5.8+) and jam to the *Loose Ends'* belay niche on a sloping ramp. **Pitch 2:** Follow the ramp up left to the buttress corner and then up right (5.4) to a ledge. **Pitch 3:** Jam a finger crack above the belay—first fingers (5.8), then excellent hands (5.7). Undercling right (5.7) below a roof to a belay ledge shared with *Loose Ends.*

Pitch 4: Move right across an easy slab and up a groove to The Cave. Belay or continue up The Cave via a slot left of a block. Finish easily to The Book's right skyline. **Rack:** Sets of Stoppers, TCUs, and cams from ½ inch to 4 inches with extra medium sizes.

7. Thindependence (5.10c) No topo. Fun link-up to *Pear Buttress, Loose Ends,* and *J-Crack* or just climb and rappel. Scramble up easy rock (4th class) on the left side of *Pear Buttress* flake to a ledge. Jam double finger cracks (5.10c) above the ledge's left side to a crack that angles up right to the first *Pear Buttress* belay. Continue up one of the above routes or descend. **Descent:** Traverse left 20 feet and climb down flakes at the buttress edge to a 2-bolt rappel station. Rappel 65 feet.

8. Stretch Marks (5.11a) Head left from the *Pear Buttress* flake and scramble up a slab to a ledge. Face climb up a seam (5.11a) to a piton. Climb a layback crack (5.10d) and chimney slot. Finish up a crack (5.9) to a 2-bolt anchor on the edge. **Descent:** Rappel 65 feet. **Rack:** TCUs, small Stoppers, small to medium cams.

9. Thinstone (5.9) Begin left of *Stretch Marks* and right of a gully. Climb an excellent thin crack in a corner to an RP-protected crux (5.9) 30 feet up. Climb up right to a chimney slot and finish up *Stretch Marks*. **Descent:**

65-foot rappel from a 2-bolt anchor. **Rack:** RPs, Stoppers, and cams to #2 Camalot.

10. Fat City (5.10c) One of Lumpy's best climbs. To start, scramble to a ledge with trees left of a left-facing dihedral. **Pitch 1:** Jam a left-leaning crack (5.8) up the center of the slab to a belay stance with bolt anchors. 100 feet. **Pitch 2:** Crux. Continue up a narrowing crack with fingerlocks (5.10a). Make an exposed hand traverse left to a niche. Thrutch through a flared slot (5.8) and jam over a roof (5.10c) to a ledge. **Pitch 3:** Layback up a right-angling crack and flake system (sustained 5.9) to a belay near The Cave. **Pitch 4:** Continue up right through The Cave and climb easier rock to the skyline ridge. **Rack:** Sets of Stoppers, TCUs, and Friends or Camalots to #4; a few RPs are handy.

11. The 44 (5.10c) *Fat City*'s companion shares its upper pitches. Begin 50 feet left of *Fat City* below a wide crack that ends at an overlap. **Pitch 1:** Climb the wide bushy crack (5.6) and then step left into a hand crack. Jam the crack (5.7) to a semihanging belay. Alternatively, belay lower at a better stance. **Pitch 2:** Jam the hand crack (5.8) to a down-pointing overlap. Layback a crack below the overlap up right to an alcove and join *Fat City* under a roof. Climb *Fat City*'s last two pitches. **Rack:** Sets of Stoppers, TCUs, and Friends or Camalots to #3.

12. George's Tree (5.9 or 5.10c) Fun stuff. Begin at a crack with a pine tree—George's tree—in it. **Pitch 1:** Jam a flared finger and hand crack (5.9). Pass a belay anchor and another steep section (5.9). Step left at the top to a belay ledge. **Pitch 2:** Step right into the crack and work up an off-width crack (5.10c) to a belay stance. For an easier pitch, climb flakes and cracks (5.5) up left before climbing right into a crack system (5.8). Follow it to a belay where the two cracks meet. **Pitch 3:** Climb the right-hand crack (5.8) for a long pitch over a headwall (5.9) to Fang Ledge, which splits the upper face. Step left a few feet and belay at an alcove. **Pitch 4:** From the alcove's right side, jam a crack (5.9) and continue up cracks to a ledge. **Pitch 5:** Climb a left-facing corner to the summit. 50 feet. **Rack:** Sets of Stoppers with double medium and large sizes, TCUs, and cams to 3 inches with double small sizes.

13. Osiris (5.7) Excellent and popular climb up the crack maze on the Pages Wall. To start, locate a chimney in a left-facing dihedral left of *George's Tree*. **Pitch 1:** Climb the chimney (5.6) to a belay ledge on the right (same as *George's Tree*). 140 feet. **Pitch 2:** From the right side of the ledge, climb left on flakes and cracks up a series of steps (5.5) to a ledge with a tree. 55 feet. **Pitch 3:** Jam a crack up a right-facing corner (5.6) or cracks to the right to double cracks (sustained 5.7) up a headwall. Belay on Fang Ledge. **Pitch 4:** Scoot left on the ledge to The Fang. Hop on top of The Fang, then follow the left crack up and over a bulging roof (5.7) and belay at a tree. **Pitch 5:** Climb easier cracks (5.3) up left to the summit, avoiding the headwall to the right. **Descent:** Scramble east and south in gullies or rappel from trees. **Rack:** Sets of Stoppers, TCUs, and cams to 3 inches with extra hand-sizes; 200-foot (60-meter) rope.

THE PEAR

The Pear is a 400-foot-high granite shield perched above the valley floor. The slabby buttress offers great friction and face routes, with most ending at low-angle slabs partway up. The Pear, popular with moderate leaders, is busy on weekends. The cliff, sheltered from the wind, is ideal for climbing during cool months.

Finding the cliff: From the Lumpy Ridge Trailhead parking area on Devils Gulch Road (GPS: N 40.396437 / W -105.512818), hike west 0.7 mile to Black Canyon Trail. Continue west for just over a mile. After passing through a gate in a barbed wire fence, look for a trail that heads northwest (GPS: N 40.403959 / W -105.539989) to the cliff base (GPS: N 40.40745 / W -105.540802).

Descent: Descent is possible from almost every route after two pitches. To descend from routes on the right slab, scramble east across a ledge system or climb easy slabs to the low-angle east ridge. From the ridge, scramble down slabs on the east side. To descend from routes left of the big left-facing dihedral, follow a walk-off ledge west from the halfway point. From the summit, locate anchors and make a 75-foot rappel north into a gully behind the top. Descend east down a gully and around the cliff's east shoulder.

Billy Westbay, a guide for Fantasy Ridge climbing school, moved to Estes Park in the early 1970s from Colorado Springs and, coupled with other guides including Douglas Snively and Dan McClure, put up a slew of hard free climbs at Lumpy in the 1970s. Some of Billy's proudest ascents were the first free ascent of the *J-Crack* headwall in 1973, led by Dan McClure; *Heavenly Journey*, a 5.10 X slab route on The Pear, in 1974 with George Hurley; and the classic *Sidetrack* on Sundance in 1975 with Mike Covington and Snively. Westbay, with John Long and Jim Bridwell, did the first one-day ascent of El Capitan's *Nose* in Yosemite Valley in 1975 and free-climbed *D1* on The Diamond in 1978 with John Bachar. Billy Westbay succumbed to cancer at age 47 in 2000.

Ian Spencer-Green on the classic slab route *Magical Chrome Plated Semi-Automatic Enema Syringe* on The Pear.

The Pear

1. Gina's Surprise (5.4 R) Fine beginner's route up a vertical dike on the slab's right side. Start below the dike. **Pitch 1:** Climb unprotected slabs to the dike and waltz upward on either side of it (left 5.5 or right 5.4) to a belay ledge with a tree. 155 feet. **Pitch 2:** Climb an easy crack up right for 80 feet to the east ridge and scramble east or continue to the summit on the easy ridge for three pitches. **Rack:** RPs, Stoppers, and TCUs.

2. Right Dihedral (5.9) Good climbing up a left-facing dihedral. **Pitch 1:** Jam and stem up a left-facing dihedral (5.9) to a belay stance where the dihedral bends left as a roof. 150 feet.

Pitch 2: Continue up the dihedral (5.7) to a ledge. **Descent:** Scramble off right to the east ridge and downclimb slabs. **Rack:** Sets of TCUs and cams to #5 Camalot.

3. Fat-Bottomed Groove (5.10d) Excellent climb. Use double ropes or lots of slings for rope drag on pitch 1. Start at a water groove below the right side of a roof band. **Pitch 1:** Chimney up the groove (5.8) to the roof or jam a hand crack (5.10c) right of the groove. Below the roof, hand traverse left along a horizontal flake and swing over (5.10d) to a belay niche. 65 feet. **Pitch 2:** Delicately edge and smear up a white dike (5.9).

Above, trend left on easier slabs to a ledge. **Pitch 3:** Climb right to the east ridge. **Descent:** Scramble down slabs. **Rack:** RPs, Stoppers, TCUs, cams to 3 inches, and a few runners.

4. The Whole Thing (5.10a) I can't believe I ate it! Begin left of *Fat-Bottomed Groove* below a notch in the roof. Scramble onto a ledge. **Pitch 1:** Stem off a tree and climb a white dike past a bolt to the roof. Clip a piton and bolt and muscle through a notch in the roof (5.10a) and belay above. **Pitch 2:** Face climb up left on a slab (5.8) and smear up a thin seam (5.10a). Climb an easier crack above (5.9), then traverse up right to a belay stance. **Pitch 3:** Climb easily up right to the east ridge. **Rack:** Sets of Stoppers, TCUs, and cams to 3 inches. RPs and extra Stoppers for pitch 2.

5. Slippage (5.9+ R) Excellent thin face moves. Scramble 60 feet to a tree right of a groove and belay. **Pitch 1:** Face climb right of the groove (5.8) to an old bolt. Work up left to a couple of short cracks to a thin corner in a break in the roof band. Work up right (5.9+) and then step back left (5.9+ R). Climb a thin crack and move left to another crack and belay. **Pitch 2:** Continue up the crack until it ends. Traverse right to a crack and climb to a left-angling ramp with a tree. Continue up right on easy terrain to the east ridge. **Rack:** RPs, Stoppers, TCUs, and small to medium cams.

6. Root of All Evil & Sibling Rivalry (5.9+) Great link-up. Begin right of a large left-facing dihedral. **Pitch 1:** Climb a slab and cracks to a thin crack. Jam the tricky crack (5.8) to the left side of a long roof. Clip a bolt and latch a jug above the roof (5.9+). Climb a crack (5.7) and belay. **Pitch 2:** Face climb up left and edge up the right side of an arête to a belay. 4 bolts to a 2-bolt belay. **Descent:** Rappel 165 feet. **Rack:** Sets of Stoppers, TCUs, and cams to #2 Friend.

7. Magical Chrome Plated Semi-Automatic Enema Syringe (5.6) Excellent and classic. Many climb the first two pitches and traverse off left. Start by scrambling (3rd Class) onto a small buttress left of a left-facing dihedral. **Pitch 1:** Jam the left crack (5.5) to a hand traverse left (5.6). Belay below a right-facing corner. **Pitch 2:** Make a tricky move above the belay and layback up a beautiful corner (5.6) to a ledge. Scramble west here or continue. **Pitch 3:** Climb a flake to a ramp left of the big dihedral. Climb the ramp (5.5) to a belay at a V-slot. **Pitch 4:** Climb the slot and jam a crack (5.6) to a ledge below the final headwall. **Pitch 5:** Traverse up right and climb a right-facing corner (5.7), then an easier headwall up left to the summit. An easier finish works under overhangs to a belay stance. Climb a short crack above (5.5) to the upper slabs. **Descent:** Rappel 75 feet off the back from a 2-bolt anchor.

8. L'Chaim (5.7) Fun climbing up the left slabs. Start below a finger crack above a roof band. **Pitch 1:** Climb a short corner on the left side of a flake to an easy white dike (5.5 R) past a tree (tie it off) to a slab (5.7 R). Belay below a crack at the right side of an overlap. 150 feet. **Pitch 2:** Climb up right and jam a perfect finger crack (5.7) to a belay ledge. Scramble off left on the ledge or continue up *MCPSAES*. **Rack:** Some RPs, set of Stoppers with extra small sizes, small to medium cams.

SUNDANCE BUTTRESS

Sundance Buttress, almost 1,000 feet high, is the tallest and most remote crag at Lumpy Ridge. Its walls are split by cracks, chimneys, and corners and divided by slabs and faces. Sundance offers everything for a marvelous climbing adventure, including wide views, excellent granite, and many classic routes. The buttress naturally divides into four sectors—from east to west are North Slabs, Turnkorner Buttress, Guillotine Wall, and Eumenides Slab. All the Sundance routes are multi-pitch affairs that require a whole day to approach, climb, and descend. Bring a rain coat in summer since thunderstorms often build in the afternoon.

For most routes, carry a rack with sets of Stoppers, TCUs, and cams to 4 inches. A 200-foot (60-meter) rope is best although a 165-foot (50-meter) rope works fine, too. Also toss a #5 Camalot on the rack for off-width cracks.

Finding the cliff: From the Lumpy Ridge Trailhead parking area on Devils Gulch Road (GPS: N 40.396437 / W -105.512818), hike west 0.7 mile to Black Canyon Trail. Continue west for just over 2 miles. A climber's trail, marked by a sign or a cairn, heads northwest up steep, wooded slopes below Turnkorner Buttress. Allow at least an hour to hike from car to cliff.

Descent: The descent from the cliff top is complex and time-consuming, and involves fourth-class downclimbing or rappels. The standard descent route scrambles north from the tops of Guillotine Wall and Turnkorner Buttress to The Saddle, a notch between Turnkorner and Guillotine. Downclimb or rappel down several short walls for 300 feet to a wooded gully. Scramble east and southeast down the gully around the North Slabs and around to the cliff base. If the weather is bad, rig rappels from trees for safety. From the top of *The Nose* and *Idiot Wind,* make two 165-foot rappels down the North Slabs to the gully.

Turnkorner Buttress

Turnkorner Buttress, on the east side of Sundance, is a huge pointed buttress with slabs on its east flank and a band of big angling roofs splitting its south face. A deep chimney system separates Turnkorner from Guillotine Wall to the west. The Sundance access trail reaches the base of Turnkorner Buttress at a huge flake.

1. The Nose (III 5.10b R) Great climb up the exposed nose of Turnkorner Buttress. Start below The Nose and left of a left-facing dihedral left of the buttress's low point. **Pitch 1:** Climb a right-angling ramp for 50 feet. Work left to a right-facing dihedral on the right side of a pillar. Jam and layback (5.9) to the pillar top. 150 feet. **Pitch 2:** Climb a right-facing flake. Face climb left (no pro) to a wide crack (5.9). Belay from two bolts on a ledge. **Pitch 3:** Climb a right-facing corner (5.7) to an A-shaped roof. Climb over the roof and follow a crack to a fixed anchor at a stance. **Pitch 4:** Work up right along a thin corner (5.9+) into an arching corner. Climb the corner to a thin seam that angles left over a bulge. Climb the seam (5.10b) and then face climb up right (5.8 R) to a groove belay. **Pitch 5:** Climb the groove to the right side of a big roof. Exit right (5.8) and follow a crack (5.7) to a belay ledge. **Pitch 6:** Climb easy rock (4th class) to a big terrace. Traverse right to descend by making two 165-foot rappels down the North Slabs or continue up. **Pitches 7 and 8:** Cruise easier runout 5th-class slabs (spots of 5.6) to the summit. **Descent:** From the top, scramble to The Saddle. See descent information above. **Rack:** Sets of Stoppers, TCUs, and cams to 3 inches with doubles in small and medium sizes; two 165-foot (50-meter) ropes.

2. Idiot Wind (III 5.10a/b) Superb, spectacular, exposed, and exciting—a great adventure. Combines *The Nose* and *Firebird*. Begin below a left-arching corner 40 feet left of *The Nose* and below a thin crack. **Pitch 1:** Jam a 40-foot finger crack (5.9) and face climb right (5.9+ R) into a left-facing corner on the left side of a pillar. Follow the corner crack (5.9) to a belay ledge atop the pillar. 160 feet. **Pitch 2:** Face climb up left from the belay (5.7 R) to an easy groove/corner. Climb a short crack to a 2-bolt belay stance (shared with *The Nose*). **Pitch 3:** Start up *The Nose*'s third pitch. Climb a crack to a roof. Climb up left (5.9+) to the right side of a long roof. Traverse up left above the roof with airy face moves (5.10a) past two bolts. End at an exposed 2-bolt belay stance on a slab. **Pitch 4:** Climb a short crack and then face climb diagonally up left (5.9) above the roof (four bolts). Jam a finger crack (5.9) to a bolt and fixed piton (possible belay). An exposed layback (5.10a) climbs past the left side of a big roof to a ledge belay. **Pitch 5:** Climb a crack (5.8) above the right side of the ledge to easier rock. Belay up right on a terrace. Traverse right to descend by making two 165-foot rappels down the North Slabs or continue up. **Pitches 6 and 7:** Continue up cracks, corners, and slabs (5.6 in spots) to the summit. **Descent:** From the top, scramble to The Saddle. See descent information above. **Rack:** Sets of Stoppers, TCUs,

and cams to 3 inches with doubles in small and medium sizes; two 165-foot (50-meter) ropes.

3. Turnkorner (III 5.10b) Intimidating Lumpy testpiece. Expect varied and strenuous climbing up the longest section of the wall. The route follows a long crack system up the middle of Turnkorner Buttress left of a large roof band. Pitches can be combined. Begin at a right-facing dihedral just left of a flake boulder 100 feet left from where the access trail meets the cliff. **Pitch 1:** Stem and jam the dihedral (5.9) to a belay on the left. **Pitch 2:** Jam a hand crack (5.8) to a flared crack (5.9) to a good belay on a ledge. **Pitch 3:** Climb a shallow corner up left (5.9), then face climb (5.9) to a left-angling ramp and belay below a roof. **Pitch 4:** Thrash up an overhanging fist crack and off-width slot (5.10b) above the left end of the ramp, then work up an off-width (5.10a) to a semihanging belay below the roof band. **Pitch 5:** Continue up the strenuous off-width crack over an imposing roof (5.10a). Avoid the off-width with scary face climbing (5.10) right of the crack. Above, grunt up a flared chimney with a hand and fist crack inside (5.9) until it ends. Step right to a belay stance. **Pitch 6:** Traverse right and jam a flared crack (5.6) to a belay on a terrace. **Pitch 7:** Angle up left to a crack (5.6) that leads to low-angle slabs or climb a crack and corner (5.8) and up left (5.9) in a left-facing angling corner to a belay ledge. **Pitch 8:** From either ledge, scramble up left on easy rock to The Saddle. **Descent:** Descend east from The Saddle. See descent information above. **Rack:** Sets of Stoppers and Camalots to #4 or equivalent, with doubles from #2 to #4 and a #5 Camalot.

4. Mr. President (III 5.10d) Strenuous crack classic. Route climbs a crack to the saddle on the left side of Turnkorner Buttress. Begin below a flared wide crack in a right-facing dihedral. **Pitch 1:** Work up the flared crack/chimney (5.9) with stems and jams in the hand crack inside the flare. Hard to protect. **Pitch 2:** Continue up the steep, thin crack as it bends right. Tricky committing moves (5.10d) lead to buckets. Step left and climb a couple of cracks (5.9) to a belay ledge. **Pitch 3:** Jam the left of two parallel cracks above (5.9) to a belay stance on the left. **Pitches 4 and 5:** Climb cracks up the big dihedral to the saddle behind Turnkorner Buttress. **Descent:** Descend east from The Saddle. See descent information above. **Rack:** Sets of Stoppers, TCUs, and cams to 3 inches.

5. Bonzo to Chain of Command (II 5.11a) Two-route link-up is an excellent outing. Begin left of *Mr. President* below a right-facing dihedral. **Pitch 1:** *Bonzo*—awesome pitch! Thin face moves (5.9) head up right to the hanging right-facing dihedral. Jam a

Sundance Buttress—Guillotine Wall

strenuous flared crack with fingers and thin hands (5.10a then 5.10b at top) up the dihedral to a headwall. Stem left to a 2-bolt stance. 110 feet. **Pitch 2:** *Chain of Command.* Face climb up left past six bolts (5.10c above third bolt) along the buttress edge. At the last bolt, clip a sling and climb to old bolts on a ledge. Continue up right 25 feet on a steep headwall (5.11a) to a 2-bolt anchor. Watch rope drag. 130 feet. **Descent:** Two double-rope rappels to the ground. **First rappel:** 130 feet to *Bonzo's* anchors. **Second rappel:** 110 feet to the ground. **Rack:** Quickdraws, Stoppers, TCUs, and Camalots from #0.5 to #2; a 70-meter rope works doubled for rappels.

Guillotine Wall

The Guillotine Wall, named for the route *Guillotine,* is the big middle wall on Sundance Buttress. It offers several mega-classic, multi-pitch moderate routes that are not only popular but also are some of Rocky Mountain National Park's best climbs. The hiking approach, however, keeps the crowds at bay, so expect lots of solitude and silence on your chosen climb. To access the routes, follow a cliff-base trail west from Turnkorner Buttress.

6. Kor's Flake (III 5.7+) 900 feet. Varied and sustained climbing and wild exposure make Layton's masterpiece one of Colorado's best 5.7 routes! Don't let the grade fool you—this is not a route for a beginning leader. Begin below a chimney capped with a chockstone left of a deep chimney. **Pitch 1:** Squeeze up the chimney (5.6) to a ledge. Continue up a crack system (5.4) to a belay ledge below Kor's Flake. **Pitch 2:** Work up a corner (5.7+) to the flake, then jam up a crack on the flake ramp to a belay stance. Don't run it farther since no good belays are higher in the wide crack. **Pitch 3:** Climb the long flake crack, which slowly widens into an off-width/squeeze chimney (5.7+). Protect with a #5 Camalot. Belay on a slab above the flake. 155 feet. **Pitch 4:** Climb up and left to a right-facing corner (5.7) to a roof passed on the left. Traverse left and jam a hand crack (5.6) to a belay ledge. 125 feet. **Pitch 5:** Climb a left-facing dihedral to a roof. Swing by it on the left (5.7) and climb cracks up left to a good ledge. 140 feet. **Pitch 6:** Climb easy rock (5.0) up a groove to a belay tree. **Descent:** Traverse right across ledges to the East Saddle descent. See descent information above. **Rack:** Set of Stoppers, set of Camalots to #5 with double #2 and #3.

"I did five routes on Sundance Buttress," said Layton Kor, "but I only got credit for three. That perturbed me. On Kor's Flake I found an old, old piton with a rappel sling on it, on the part they call *Kor's Flake*. I didn't name it that. Very enjoyable climb. I've done it six or seven times."

7. Mainliner (III 5.9-) 900 feet. One of Lumpy's best and most popular long routes with exposure, lots of easy climbing, and short cruxes. Hike along the cliff base past *Turnkorner's* big roof and a couple of chimneys. Start below a large open dihedral. **Pitch 1:** Climb up left in cracks (5.7), then work up right in a dihedral (5.7) to a belay stance. **Pitch 2:** Climb a corner above, then face climb up left and follow cracks (5.7) to a small roof (5.8) and left-angling crack. Finish at a good belay ledge. **Pitch 3:** Climb up (5.6) to a groove with two opposing corners. Stem the corners (5.9) to a ledge. Climb up a pod and jam a finger crack over a bulge (5.9) to a good crack (5.7). End at a sloping ledge below a right-facing corner. **Pitch 4:** Start up the dihedral (5.8), then climb up left and belay on a ledge below a slot. **Pitch 5:** Climb the chimney slot (5.7) and follow cracks to a belay ledge. From the ledge, either climb up cracks and work right into a slabby corner or traverse right onto a wide terrace. Scramble right for the descent. **Descent:** Traverse right across ledges to the East Saddle descent. See descent info above. **Rack:** Sets of Stoppers, TCUs, and Camalots or equivalent to #4. A 200-foot (60-meter) rope is handy.

8. Sidetrack (III 5.9) 900 feet. A great Sundance moderate. Start left of *Mainliner* and left of a large flake. **Pitch 1:** Climb thin cracks up a shallow right-facing corner to face climbing (5.8+) to a small belay ledge below a slot. **Pitch 2:** Work up the slot (5.9) to a roof. Pass it on the left and climb a crack (5.8) to a belay ledge. **Pitch 3:** Jam a 4-inch crack (5.8) to a belay ledge down left of *Mainliner's* second belay. **Pitch 4:** Climb a crack system (5.6) to a good belay ledge. **Pitch 5:** Great climbing! Don't bail right to *Mainliner*. Climb a steep thin crack (5.9) to an A-frame roof. Stem and jam over the roof (5.9) and climb to a ledge above. **Pitch 6:** Climb up right and join *Mainliner*. Climb a slot (5.7) then up easier rock to a belay ledge. **Descent:** Traverse right across ledges to the East Saddle descent. **Rack:** Sets of Stoppers, TCUs, and Camalots to #4.

9. Grapevine (III 5.8+) Classic Layton Kor route on the wall's far left side. Start left of *Sidetrack* below a finger crack. **Pitch 1:** Jam the crux finger crack (5.8+) up right to a groove corner system right of some orange lichen. Climb a left-facing corner to a roof, then climb up left (5.8) to a belay ledge. **Pitch 2:** Jam a fist crack (5.7) to a chimney. Work up the awesome chimney (5.6) to a good ledge. Get pro in cracks in the back of the chimney. **Pitch 3:** Climb an easy corner up left to a ledge. Face climb directly up right (5.9 R) or climb an easy crack on the left and then work up right (5.4) to a vertical crack. Jam the crack (5.7) to a big ledge below a

Sundance Buttress—Guillotine Wall

left-facing dihedral. **Pitch 4:** Climb the left-facing dihedral (5.7) until it steepens. Work up cracks to the left (5.8+) or climb directly up the steep pumpy dihedral (5.8+) to a belay ledge up right. **Pitch 5:** Climb cracks (5.5) in the face above to a belay ledge. **Pitch 6:** Continue up more slabby cracks (5.4) to the summit. **Descent:** Scramble down right to the East Saddle descent. **Rack:** Sets of Stoppers and cams to #3 Camalot (double #2 and #3 Camalots) and a few hexentric nuts.

Rob Masters leads the second pitch of *Camel Toes* up the middle of MacGregor Slab.

6

MacGregor Slab

MacGregor Slab is an impressive 600-foot-high granite shield pasted on the southwest slopes of Mac-Gregor Mountain, northwest of Estes Park. The southwest-facing slab, looming above the Fall River Entrance to Rocky Mountain National Park, offers a great selection of moderate multi-pitch routes up cracks, corners, and slabs. The slab's center has the hardest climbs, tricky enough to challenge most climbers, while the right and left sides present fairly easy routes.

MacGregor's featured granite is made for climbing with lots of flakes, edges, cracks, dihedrals, and smears. The routes can be hard to follow and confusing, with lots of arching corner systems. Take these route descriptions with a grain of salt and realize that you may not follow the same line, but no problem—MacGregor's terrain is well protected, very climbable, and almost never harder than 5.8 climbing.

Finding the cliff: See map on page vii. Drive northwest from Estes Park on US 34 (Fall River Road) for about 5 miles to the Fall River Visitor Center, just before the Fall River Entrance to Rocky Mountain National Park. Park in the visitor center parking lot (GPS: N 40.401982 / W -105.586893). MacGregor Slab is obvious on the mountainside above. Cross the highway and hike up a road past the Della-Terra Lodge. Find a climber's trail that begins right of a couple of buildings and follow it up a ravine to the base of the wall. Allow thirty minutes to hike from car to cliff.

Descent: Descend from the summit by hiking off the back on easy slabs into a gully that drops down the east side of the cliff. Look for an easy spot to scramble down or rappel from a convenient tree into the gully. A good descent is also down the left side of the dome, although some blown-down trees are found. The last couple pitches of most routes are very easy, so many parties escape to the right or left before reaching the top. There is the illusion of safety at the top and hazardous falls are possible. After climbing *Left Standard,* it's easy to traverse left on a big ledge to escape. From routes in the middle of the cliff, rappel down *Camel Toes* in the middle of the slab from the top of pitch 4 with double 200-foot (60-meter) ropes.

1. Left Standard (II 5.3) Excellent—best easy route in the park. Lots of variations since the terrain is so moderate. Hike along the cliff base to the far left side of the wall and start below a clean slab and prominent double roofs. **Pitch 1:** Two ways to go. Climb a right-facing corner past a stunted pine (5.3) to a belay ledge at a tree. Or start left of the corner and smear up a nice slab (5.3) to the same belay. **Pitch 2:** Climb up right along a long right-angling corner (5.3). Belay at a stance below a small roof. **Pitch 3:** Pass the roof on its left and climb cracks to a belay ledge at a tree. Scramble up left onto a ledge system with trees and downclimb into the gully to the left or continue up. **Pitches 4 and 5:** Climb easy cracks to the summit.

2. Left Standard Variation (5.5)
From the top of pitch 1 on *Left Standard,* climb up right-facing corners to the obvious roof. Work past the roof and belay on a ledge above or continue to the tree-covered terrace.

Rocky Mountain National Park is the mother of four great rivers—Colorado, Cache la Poudre, Big Thompson, and St. Vrain. More than 150 lakes in the park reflect sky and cloud, and almost 500 miles of streams and rivers tumble down valleys and canyons. One-third of the park lies in the Alpine life zone, the chilly land above the trees where summer visits for only two months a year. Explore the Alpine zone by driving 48-mile Trail Ridge Road, the highest paved highway in the United States, and hiking its interpretative trails.

3. Overhang (II 5.7) Excellent and fun. This two-pitch start avoids the runout second pitch of *Lubrication*. Start at the left center of the face by scrambling out right on a ledge with trees. **Pitch 1:** Climb a slab above a flake to a right-facing corner (5.6). Belay on a stance. 150 feet. **Pitch 2:** Work up corners and slabs (5.7) to a belay below an overlap. **Pitches 3 to 6:** Climb *Lubrication* to the summit.

4. Lubrication (II 5.9 R) Great route! Just a bit runout on pitch 2. Begin left of the low point of the face. Scramble up left (3rd class) on a low-angle slab to a 2-bolt belay ledge. **Pitch 1:** Climb a slab (5.8) past a couple of bolts to a belay at a tree on a ledge. **Pitch 2:** Smear carefully up left along a runout polished groove (5.9 R) to a crack to a belay stance below an overlap. **Pitch 3:** Climb up and over the overlap above (5.7). Trend up left on flakes (5.4) and belay at a crack. **Pitch 4:** Pull past an overlap above and climb up right on flakes and cracks (5.6) to a stance at a small tree. **Pitch 5:** Climb a groove and shallow corner up right (5.5) to a belay stance on a horizontal dike. **Pitch 6:** Climb a right-facing corner (5.5) past a tree to the left. Continue up a corner to a convenient belay ledge. **Pitch 7:** Finish up easy cracks and corners (5.4) to a belay. Scramble to the summit. **Rack:** Sets of Stoppers and cams to 3 inches, 200-foot (60-meter) rope.

5. Camel Toes (II 5.9+) Excellent bolted route up the midsection. Look around for the bolts as you climb. Start left of the end of the approach trail below a low-angle slab on the left side. **Pitch 1:** Climb the slab (5.7) to a belay at a tree with rappel slings. 4 bolts. 125 feet. **Pitch 2:** Friction up the sustained slab (four 5.9 cruxes) past a couple of overlaps to an anchor. 13 bolts to 2-bolt anchor. 175 feet. **Pitch 3:** Climb up right past a couple of bolts, then pull over a roof (5.7) with good holds and climb to a horizontal crack. Smear past a couple of bolts (5.9+) to easier rock and a horizontal crack. Finish up a nice slab to anchors up left. 5 bolts to 2-bolt anchor. 190 feet. **Pitch 4:** Climb a short right-facing corner, then climb a fun slab (5.8) to anchors. 4 bolts to 2-bolt anchor. 155 feet. **Pitch 5:** Work up right to a short headwall (5.4) to a tree on a ledge. 140 feet. **Pitch 6:** From the tree, climb up left in a groove (5.6) to easier low-angle climbing to the cliff top and rappel anchors. 140 feet. **Descent:** Rappel the route with double 200-foot (60-meter) ropes. Best to rap from the top of pitch 5. Or descend the backside from the summit. **Rack:** Small assortment of Stoppers, set of TCUs, #0.75 to #3 Camalots, six 2-foot slings, quick-draws, 200-foot (60-meter) rope.

6. Direct (II 5.7) Fun, popular, and long. Begin at a left-facing corner system left of the lowest part of the slab.

Pitch 1: Climb left-facing corners (5.7) to a good ledge on the left or climb easy rock to the left. **Pitch 2:** Continue up a large left-facing corner (5.7) to a belay ledge on the left. **Pitch 3:** Work up left along a hanging overlap until you can pull over (5.7) to a stance. Face climb up right to a small belay stance. **Pitch 4:** Friction up a nice slab (5.6) to some right-facing corners. Climb the one on the right (5.6) and work up left onto a slab to a belay at a horizontal crack system. **Pitch 5:** Climb an open right-facing corner (5.5) to a tree. Continue up right on easier slabs to a convenient belay ledge. **Pitch 6:** Scamper up cracks and slabs to the summit. You can avoid the top two pitches by traversing right on a ledge system to the right skyline and the east-side descent route. **Rack:** Sets of Stoppers and cams to 3 inches; a 200-foot (60-meter) rope is best.

7. Indirect (II 5.7) Good climb up the slab's middle. Begin below a left-facing dihedral system. **Pitch 1:** Climb a broken dihedral (bit of 5.7) to a belay stance. **Pitch 2:** Continue up the clean corner (5.7) until it ends. Climb a crack up right (5.6) to a horizontal belay ledge. **Pitch 3:** Climb a left-facing corner (5.7), then climb an easier left-trending crack to a ledge with trees. **Pitch 4:** Move left and climb cracks and slab to an overlap. Move past it (5.7) and continue up right to a belay ledge below an arching roof. **Pitch 5:** Climb past the left side of the arch (5.7) to a big tree on a ledge. Exit right on the ledge to the descent route or climb an easy pitch to the summit. **Rack:** Sets of Stoppers and cams to 3 inches; a 200-foot (60-meter) rope is best.

8. Right Standard (II 5.6) Popular classic climb. Start below a left-facing corner system right of *Indirect.* **Pitch 1:** Climb the broken corner system (5.6), passing a roof on its right side. Scramble up right and belay at a couple of trees. An alternative start goes up the first corner on *Indirect,* then escapes right onto ledges. **Pitch 2:** Climb cracks up a slab to a belay at a horizontal crack. **Pitch 3:** Smear up a fun slab (5.6) to a left-facing flake. Continue up right in a left-facing corner (5.6) to a belay at trees. **Pitch 4:** More good slab climbing goes up right past a couple of small overlaps to a belay on a good ledge. Scramble off right to the descent route. **Rack:** Sets of Stoppers and cams to 3 inches; a 200-foot (60-meter) rope is best.

7.

Jurassic Park

Jurassic Park, a jumble of granite fins, slabs, and faces, perches high on a mountainside above Lily Lake, south of Estes Park. A varied selection of single-pitch, bolted sport routes ascend the compact area's half-dozen cliffs. Besides offering fun climbing, Jurassic Park also boasts some of the best climbing views in the Rocky Mountain National Park area, with stunning vistas of Longs Peak to the south.

Jurassic Park lies just northeast and outside of the national park boundary in Roosevelt National Forest, while Lily Lake, the access trail, and the parking area are in Rocky Mountain National Park. National park restrictions, including no dogs, applies to the access trail. No fees are charged by the park to either hike or park at Lily Lake.

Finding the area: Drive south from Estes Park on CO 7 to the Lily Lake parking area on the right (west) side of the highway (GPS: N 40.306695 / W -105.537746). Parking is also on the east side of the highway. Before

Jurassic Park Overview

Jurassic Park

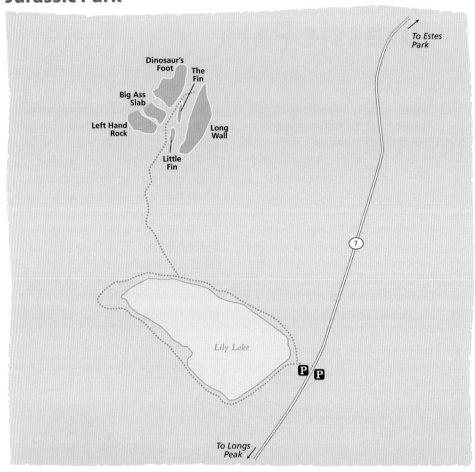

leaving your car, look northwest to the upper slopes of Lily Mountain and locate Jurassic Park's obvious cliffs. Hike west along a good trail on the north side of the lake to a broad meadow with a bench on Lily Lake's northwest side. Go right and hike up a steep trail to the Lily Ridge Trail. Cross it and continue steeply uphill on a loose climber's path to Jurassic Park. Hiking time from car to cliff is twenty to thirty minutes.

LEFT HAND ROCK

Left Hand Rock is the first major formation on the left (west) side of the approach gully and trail. Identify the cliff by a deep chimney that splits the face. The left route climbs a steep buttress above an obvious roof, while the right routes ascend a slabby spur.

Descent: Descend off all routes by rappelling or lowering from bolt anchors.

1. Gilded Lily (5.9) Begin beneath a low roof on the left side of the face. Pass the roof on the right and friction up a thin delicate slab to easier rock. Finish up steep rock. 9 bolts to 2-bolt anchor. 90 feet.

2. Dark Days (5.8-) Work up the deep chimney that divides the wall. **Rack:** Small to large cams.

3. Unknown (5.2) Climb up left to a low-angle rib. Follow it to a high bolt, then traverse right to anchors. 9 bolts to 2-bolt anchor. 95 feet.

4. T-Rect (5.7+) Climb up left to a groove. Climb the shallow groove and then move up right to anchors. Watch the runout between bolts 2 and 3. 5 bolts to 2-bolt anchor. 80 feet.

5. Triceratops (5.8- R) On the right side of Left Hand Rock. Climb a slabby face to a bulge. Pull over (5.8-) on a flake. 5 bolts to 2-bolt anchor.

Left Hand Rock

The Little Fin

THE LITTLE FIN

The Little Fin is a west-facing wall directly opposite Left Hand Rock on the east side of the access gully. A couple of fun moderate climbs are on the cliff. Access it by hiking to Left Hand Rock and following a short trail right to the cliff base.

Descent: Descend off routes by rappelling or lowering from bolt anchors.

1. Byrontosaurus (5.8-) Climb to a high first bolt, then pull flakes and edges up left to anchors. 7 bolts to 2-bolt anchor.

2. Purgatorius (5.8) Climb up and over a small roof, then trend up right to anchors. 7 bolts to 2-bolt anchor.

BIG ASS SLAB

Big Ass Slab is the second formation reached on the left (west) along the access trail from the lake. This east-facing slab offers fun bolt-protected routes on clean compact rock as well as great views of Longs Peak. Use a 200-foot (60-meter) rope on all routes and make sure your belayer pays attention when lowering you. All the routes start by the trail, with the first one on the far left side of the wall.

Descent: Descend off all routes by rappelling or lowering from bolt anchors.

1. Coloradoddity (5.6) Excellent and fun route with great views on the left side of the slab. Good beginner lead. Climb a long, sweeping, low-angle rib to high anchors. 10 bolts to 2-bolt anchor. 95 feet. **Rack:** Use a 200-foot (60-meter) rope.

2. Stout Blue Vein (5.8+) Start on a ledge below the first bolt. Climb up, then make a cruxy traverse right. Follow bolts to high anchors. 7 bolts to 2-bolt anchor. 95 feet.

3. Critical Morass (5.10d) One of Jurassic's best climbs. Excellent

friction climbing up a clean slab. Climb the slab with thin sustained smears to pockets. Use tricky feet and small crimps to surmount the crux. Finish over a high bulge to easy climbing to a ledge. 9 bolts to 2-bolt anchor. 100 feet.

4. Assomosis (5.9+) Start right of *Critical Morass.* Climb a crack in a left-facing flake to a bolt, then climb up left to a ledge. Smear upward following bolts. 5 bolts to 2-bolt anchor. 100 feet. **Rack:** TCUs and cams to 2 inches.

Big Ass Slab

Leigha Powers cruises
Coloradoddity at Jurassic Park.

DINOSAUR'S FOOT

Dinosaur's Foot is the largest climbing formation at Jurassic Park, with bolted routes on the left side of its east face and popular topropes on the right side.

Finding the cliff: The east-facing cliff is on the left (west) side of a corridor that splits the area and is the third major formation encountered on the approach trail. A brushy gully divides it from Big Ass Slab. Access the Toprope Wall by scrambling left across the top of the cliff and then carefully downclimbing to bolt anchors on the cliff edge—tie into a rope for safety.

Descent: Descend off all routes by rappelling or lowering from bolt anchors.

1. Index Toe (5.8+) Great fun and well protected. Left route on the face. Climb a blunt slabby rib to an insecure crux and difficult clip at bolt 7. Finish with easier but runout climbing to anchors with a view. 9 bolts to 2-bolt anchor. 95 feet.

2. Middle Toe (5.9-) Excellent and fun—one of the best! On the next panel right of *Index Toe*. Dicey moves off the ground lead directly up the slabby toe to a thin crux at bolt 6 and a horizontal crack. Finish with fun moves on steep rock. 9 bolts to 2-bolt anchor. 95 feet.

3. Copradelite (5.9+) Good climbing. Work up the right side of the *Middle Toe* pillar just left of a chimney system. 9 bolts to 2-bolt anchor.

4. Heel Toe (5.7) Climb a flaring chimney and crack right of *Middle Toe* until it ends, then move up left to a 2-bolt anchor. **Rack:** Medium to large cams.

5. Dino Dung (5.10a) Begin below the chimney. Climb up right on a rib and then move left and climb on the chimney's right outside edge. 7 bolts to 2-bolt anchor. 90 feet.

Dinosaur's Foot

Dinosaur's Foot

The next four routes are on the east face of a semidetached pillar.

6. Little Toe Jam (5.11a) Start uphill from *Dino Dung* on the left side of the pillar. Face climb up a short steep face. 4 bolts to 2-bolt anchor. 40 feet.

7. Pocket Full of Cryptonite (5.12a) Stick-clip bolt 1 and then crimp small edges to the third bolt. Finish with easier moves. 3 bolts to 2-bolt anchor.

8. Joint Venture (5.8) On the right side of the semidetached pillar. Climb vertical rock to a final bulge. 5 bolts to 2-bolt anchor.

9. Strategery (5.7) Right of the pillar. Climb a slab, then move up left to an easy groove. 4 bolts to 2-bolt anchor.

10. Toprope Wall (5.7–5.8) The face on the far right side of Dinosaur's Foot. Can be busy with guided parties. Locate bolt anchors on the cliff top. Access the anchors by going right and scrambling along the cliff top, then downclimb to the bolts. Use a rope for protection.

11. Toprope Wall Crack (5.7) Jam, layback, and face climb up a fun curving crack on the Toprope Wall. Finish at a bolt anchor.

Ian Spencer-Green gripping the *Edge of Time* on The Fin.

route hidden on
left side of arête

THE FIN

The Fin is the most striking and beautiful rock formation at Jurassic Park. The formation is exactly that—a long narrow fin. A couple of fine sport routes ascend the vertical west face, while the *Edge of Time*, The Fin's best route, climbs the formation's north end. The route, ascending a perfect sharp arête, offers stellar views of Longs Peak to the southwest and a great photo opportunity for a hero shot.

Finding the cliff: The Fin is along the corridor that divides Jurassic Park's formations. Hike past Big Ass Slab to Dinosaur's Foot on the left. The Fin is on the right, directly across the corridor from Dinosaur's Foot. The two routes right of #1, not included here, are *Unknown V* (5.11a) and *CG's Naked Fun Time* (5.10b).

Descent: Descend off all routes by lowering from bolt anchors or by scrambling off the backside from the summit.

1. Dynamometer (5.11b) Interesting climbing with a crux dyno near the top. Second route from the right side. Start just left of a small pine tree. Grab pockets past a couple of bolts and then plug a cam in a pocket. Continue up good rock with flexible flake handholds to the high dyno. Finish at an anchor above. 8 bolts to 2-bolt chain anchor. 90 feet. **Descent:** Rappel or lower from chains. **Rack:** Small and medium cams.

2. Andrology (5.11d/5.12a) A long, pumpy face route on great stone just right of the arête. Face climb (5.10a) up to a section of pockets and sandy huecos. Crank up left (5.11b) on steep rock to the top. 7 bolts to 2-bolt chain anchor. 90 feet. **Descent:** Rappel or lower from chains. **Rack:** Medium cams.

3. Edge of Time (5.9) Classic climbing, scenic views, and spectacular

The history of the *Edge of Time* is obscure. Rumor has it that Layton Kor and Ray Northcutt top-roped the arête in the early 1960s, but I asked Layton and he doesn't remember climbing it. "I might have climbed it," says Kor, "but I don't remember—I climbed a lot of stuff back then." The first known top-rope ascents were by Bill Morck and Justin Kraemer in June, 1987, and shortly thereafter by Bernard and Robert Gillett. In the late summer of 1987, Morck hand-drilled two bolts on lead and then lowered down. Mike Clinton finished the pitch, hammering a couple pitons higher. On mountainproject .com, Morck remembers naming it: "After smoking a 'fatty,' we somewhat lamely came up with the name *Edge of Time*—it had to be the edge of something."

position. Often toproped. A good but tricky lead. Begin below the left side of the obvious prow. Make thin face moves past the first bolt, then romp up the arête to a final crux. 4 bolts and a piton to anchors atop the route.

4. Lost Time (5.7+) Start 10 feet left of *Edge of Time*. Work up a right-facing flake to a bolt above. Continue up the face above, past a couple more spaced bolts to anchors. 3 bolts to 2-bolt anchor. **Rack:** Small to medium cams.

5. East of Eden (5.9 R) A toprope route 25 feet left of *Edge of Time*. Find anchors on top. It has been led.

LONG WALL

Long Wall sits atop Jurassic Park, just northeast of The Fin. The west-facing cliff offers a few leads and a bunch of fun toprope climbs.

Finding the cliff: Hike up the access gully through Jurassic Park. Continue past The Fin and its north arête and turn right. Long Wall is a couple hundred feet to the northeast. **Descent:** Scramble north from the top of the cliff.

1. Your Possible Pasts (5.6) Start left of a tree. Face climb 20 feet to a crack. Follow it to a cliff-top gear belay. **Rack:** Stoppers and small to medium cams.

2. Another Brick in the Wall (5.7 R) Begin 20 feet left of the tree. Lead or toprope the face. Horizontal cracks provide gear placements. **Rack:** Small to medium cams.

3. Unknown (5.8) Face climb up right past bolts to 2-bolt anchor. Cram cams in horizontal cracks for extra pro.

Long Wall

descend left

Combat Rock

8.

Combat Rock

Combat Rock, a south-facing 250-foot-high cliff, perches on the north side of Bobcat Gulch, a steep canyon that drops south to the narrow valley of the North Fork of the Big Thompson River between Loveland and Estes Park. The crag, a shield composed of hard granite, yields excellent climbs that edge up steep slabs, jam discontinuous crack systems, and swing over blocky roofs. The easily accessible cliff, approached by a short trail, is sunny and sheltered, making it an ideal outing in autumn or spring.

Most of the routes are bolted, but carry a small rack with Stoppers, TCUs, and small to medium Friends to supplement bolts. Horizontal seams and shallow cracks offer lots of creative gear placements for additional pro.

Getting there: Combat Rock is reached on US 34 from Loveland and I-25 to the east or Estes Park to the west. From Loveland, drive up US 34 through Big Thompson Canyon

for 17 miles to Drake, or drive 13 miles down US 34 from Estes Park to Drake. Turn west at Drake on Devils Gulch Road (GPS: N 40.432055 / W -105.340731) and follow it for 0.5 mile to Cedar Park Road (FR 128), the first dirt road on the right or north (GPS: N 40.433525 / W -105.345782). Follow the road up switchbacks for 0.8 mile and park in a large pull-off on the north side of the road past a road cut and directly across from Combat Rock (GPS: N 40.440228 / W -105.342990). Follow a trail that begins at the parking area. Descend across Bobcat Gulch and hike up the opposite canyon slope to the cliff base. Hiking time is ten minutes.

Descent: Descend by lowering or rappelling from bolt anchors or by hiking down either side of the crag. Double ropes are needed for almost all the rappels. Double-check the pitch lengths to make sure you have enough cord to lower or rappel on single pitches.

Ian Spencer-Green fighting with *GI Joe* at Combat Rock.

1. Arkansas Patriot aka Wondering Where the Lions Are (5.9+)
Fun climb on the left edge. Climb a diagonal crack up right to a bolt, then climb a steep slab and dike to anchors. 3 bolts to 2-bolt anchor. 75 feet. **Descent:** Rappel or lower from anchors. **Rack:** Stoppers and Aliens.

2. Rambo Santa (5.7) Popular and fun. Start 45 feet right of *Arkansas Patriot* aka *Wondering Where the Lions Are*. Run it out 40 feet (5.5) to a bolt, then smear and edge up a clean slab to anchors. Place gear in horizontal cracks. 5 bolts to 2-bolt anchor. 165 feet. **Descent:** Rappel with two ropes or scramble off left (4th class). **Rack:** Stoppers and small to medium cams.

3. DMZ (5.8 R) Good but runout climbing up the slab. Begin right of *Rambo Santa* below the left side of some roofs. Climb past a couple of good bolts, then smear up runout rock (5.6 R) to an old bolt (back up with a small cam). Crank the crux and climb up left to *Rambo Santa*'s anchors. **Descent:** Rappel with two ropes or scramble off left (4th class). **Rack:** TCUs and small cams.

4. Tree Roof (5.8 R) Fun roof problem. Climb an easy slab to an obvious 5-foot roof, pull over on buckets, and belay at a tree. **Descent:** Rappel 50 feet or continue (5.7 R) to a 2-bolt anchor on *Diagonal* or *Rambo Santa*. **Rack:** #2 and #3 Camalots.

5. Pearl Harbor (5.10d) Good climbing up the central slab. Begin right of *Tree Roof*. **Pitch 1:** Climb an easy slab to a bolt, then work up thin moves (5.10b) to a roof. Pull over the roof (5.9+) and climb an easier slab to anchors up right on *Diagonal*'s crack. 6 bolts to 2-bolt anchor. 150 feet. **Pitch 2:** Climb perfect granite with edges and smears past a crux (5.10a) at bolt 2 and a high tricky crux above bolt 5. Finish up left at a 2-bolt anchor. 6 bolts to 2-bolt anchor. 130 feet. **Descent:** Do a third easy pitch to the top or make two rappels with double ropes down the route. **Rack:** Light rack with TCUs and small to medium cams.

6. Eight Clicks to Saigon (5.10d) Excellent. **Pitch 1:** Climb a 3-bolt slab (5.9) to a roof. Step over it (5.10c) and smear to *Diagonal*. Belay from gear here or move up left to a 2-bolt anchor. 6 bolts to 2-bolt anchor. 100 feet. **Pitch 2:** Face climb up right past a couple of bolts then up to a long roof. Pull past its right side (5.9) and climb up left on easier slabs and cracks (5.7) to the cliff top or work up left (5.7 R) to *Pearl Harbor*'s top anchor. A fine well-protected combo climbs *Eight Clicks to Saigon*'s first pitch and *Pearl Harbor*'s second. **Descent:** Scramble down the left side from the top or make two double-rope rappels down *Pearl Harbor*. **Rack:** Stoppers, TCUs, and small to medium cams.

Combat Rock—Right Side

7. Ain't Nobody Here but Us Chickens (5.11d) Start 25 feet down left of *Diagonal*. Climb a moderate left-facing corner to a slab. Crimp thin edges up a blank slab to a crux at bolt 3. Work up right to a small tree in a crack and a big ledge above. 3 bolts to 2-bolt anchor. 85 feet. **Descent:** Rappel from anchors. **Rack:** Stoppers and #3 Camalot.

8. Across Enemy Lines (5.11b) Just left of *Diagonal*. Climb a thin slab to the *Diagonal* crack, then climb up right over an interesting roof (5.11b/c). Work up steep rock (5.10b) to a good ledge. 6 bolts to 2-bolt anchor. A second pitch with sustained 5.11 and a 5.12b crux climbs above the ledge then up right along an arch to anchors. **Descent:** Rappel 85 feet. **Rack:** Stoppers and medium cams.

9. Diagonal (5.9) Classic crack climb that follows an obvious left-diagonaling crack system. **Pitch 1:** Jam a leaning finger crack up a left-angling corner to a sketch section with foot smears (5.9). Pass a tree to a ledge and corner. Step left and follow diagonal cracks up left to a belay ledge below a pointed roof. Use long slings to avoid rope drag on this long pitch or break it in half with a bolted belay. **Pitch 2:** Climb up right under the right-angling roof (5.9) to a flake at its end. Pull past and climb easily to a 2-bolt anchor. 100 feet. Alternatively, climb easy rock out the left side of the roof. **Descent:**

Climb to the top and scramble off left or make two double-rope rappels. **Rack:** Sets of Stoppers, TCUs, and small to medium cams. Two 200-foot (60-meter) ropes work best.

10. Blood for Oil (5.12b) Combat's best hard route. **Pitch 1:** Crimp and smear past the first two bolts (5.12b) to easier terrain and a ledge. Continue up an ultrathin slab to more cruxes (5.12a and 5.11d) and anchors below a roof. 9 bolts to 2-bolt anchor. 160 feet. **Pitch 2:** Spectacular climbing threads through double roofs (5.11) to a final crux (5.12a). Finish up a seam to anchors. 5 bolts to 2-bolt anchor. 85 feet. **Descent:** Rappel route with double ropes. **Rack:** TCUs and small to medium cams.

11. No More War (5.10a) Good jamming to thin face moves. Jam a flared hand crack (5.8) to a small tree. Continue up a water streak to a short finger crack. Finish with dicey smears (5.10a) to a shelf. Move left to anchors. 2 bolts to 2-bolt anchor. 160 feet. **Descent:** Rappel with double ropes. **Rack:** Stoppers, TCUs, and small cams.

12. Front Lines (5.10d) Classic route with devious but good pro. **Pitch 1:** Climb thin offset cracks (5.9+) past a bolt to a narrow roof. Move up right and climb a streaked left-facing corner (5.8) to a belay stance below roofs. **Pitch 2:** Traverse a few feet right and climb a thin crack through two tricky, hard-to-protect overlaps (5.10d). Motor up easy rock to a belay at a dead tree. **Descent:** Traverse left along a shelf to a 2-bolt anchor. Make two rappels (85 feet and 160 feet) down *Blood for Oil.* **Rack:** Double sets of RPs and small Stoppers, medium to large Stoppers, TCUs, small to medium cams, extra 2-foot slings.

13. Lizzard Warrior (5.10d) Superb sport route. Climb to bolt 2 on the right (5.10a) or directly (5.11b), then work up a steep slab with crisp edges to a crux (5.10d) at bolt 4. Finish at anchors below a roof. 5 bolts to 2-bolt anchor. 80 feet. **Descent:** Rappel or lower from anchors.

14. GI Joe (5.9+) Excellent but tricky moves above bolts. Start below a large roof. Grab good edges and flakes up the face to anchors below the roof. 4 bolts to 2-bolt anchor. 75 feet. **Descent:** Rappel or lower from anchors.

15. Nuclear Polka (5.10a) On the far right side. **Pitch 1:** Climb a thin left-facing corner with two cruxes to a belay stance above the right side of a big roof. **Pitch 2:** Smear a slab up left to a small roof. Jam a hand crack (5.9) to an easier crack to the cliff top. **Descent:** Scramble down the left side of the cliff. **Rack:** RPs, small Stoppers, small to medium cams.

Extreme weather characterizes Rocky Mountain National Park. As you rise in elevation, the air temperature cools about 3 degrees Fahrenheit every 1,000 feet in height. Park wind speeds reach as high as the 201-mile-per-hour gust recorded atop Longs Peak. Snow falls in every month of the year. Come prepared, even in summer, for bad weather. The day can change in 15 minutes from warm and sunny to a raging thunderstorm with lightning and snow. Bring The Ten Essentials and stay warm, dry, and safe.

Climbing Equipment & Gyms

Boulder Rock Club
2829 Mapleton Ave.
Boulder, CO 80301
(303) 447-2804

Estes Park Mountain Shop
2050 Big Thompson Ave.
Estes Park, CO 80517
(970) 586-6548
http://estesparkmountainshop.com

Evo Rock & Fitness
1754 Dogwood St.
Louisville, CO 80027
(303) 317-3770
www.evorock.com

Icebox Mountain Sports
505 Zerex Ave.
Fraser, CO 80442
(970) 722-7780
www.iceboxmtnsports.com

Jax Outdoor Gear
1200 N. College Ave.
Fort Collins, CO 80524
(970) 221-0544
www.jaxmercantile.com/
jax-fort-collins-outdoor-gear-store

950 East Eisenhower Blvd.
Loveland, CO 80537
(970) 776-4540
www.jaxmercantile.com/jax-loveland-
outdoor-gear-ranch-home-store

900 S US 287
Lafayette, CO 80026
(720) 266-6160
www.jaxmercantile.com/
jax-lafayette-outdoor-gear-store

5005 W. 120th Ave.
Broomfield, Colorado 80020
(303) 439-1000
www.jaxmercantile.com/jax-broom
field-outdoor-gear-ranch-home

Komito Boots
235 W. Riverside Dr.
Estes Park, CO 80517
(970) 586-5391

The Mountain Shop
172 N. College Ave.
Fort Collins, CO 80524
(970) 493-5720
www.themountainshop.com

Movement Gym
2845 Valmont Rd.
Boulder, CO 80301
(303) 443-1505
https://movementgyms.com

Neptune Mountaineering
633 S. Broadway
Boulder, CO 80305
(303) 499-8866
www.neptunemountaineering.com

The North Face
1129 Pearl St.
Boulder, CO 80302
(303) 449-1760
www.thenorthface.com

REI
1789 28th St.
Boulder, CO 80301
(303) 583-9970
www.rei.com/stores/boulder

REI
4025 S. College Ave.
Fort Collins, CO 80525
(970) 223-0123
www.rei.com/stores/fort-collins

The Spot Bouldering Gym
3240 Prairie Ave.
Boulder, CO 80301
(303) 379-8806
www.thespotgym.com

Wilderness Exchange
2401 15th St., Suite 100
Denver CO 80202
(303) 964-0708
www.wildernessx.com

Climbing Guides
Colorado Mountain School
341 Moraine Ave.
Estes Park, CO 80517
(970) 387-8944
https://coloradomountainschool
.com/

Estes Park Mountain Shop
2050 Big Thompson Ave.
Estes Park, CO 80517
 (970) 586-6548
www.estesparkmountainshop.com/
guided-rock-climbing

Front Range Climbing Company
1370 Windmill Ave.
Colorado Springs, CO 80904
719-632-5822 or (866) 404-3721
www.frontrangeclimbing.com

Management Agencies
Rocky Mountain National Park
1000 US 36
Estes Park, CO 80517
(970) 586-1206
www.nps.gov/romo

**Rocky Mountain National Park
Wilderness Office**
(970) 586-1242

**Longs Peak Climbing Conditions
Report**
www.nps.gov/romo/planyourvisit/
longspeak.htm

**Rocky Mountain National Park
Campground Reservations**
Online: www.recreation.gov
Toll free: (877) 444-6777
International: (518) 885-3639

Estes Park Information

Estes Park Convention & Visitors Bureau

Estes Park Visitors Center
500 Big Thompson Ave.
Estes Park, CO 80517
(800) 443-7837 or (970) 577-9900
www.visitestespark.com

Medical Services

Estes Park Health

555 Prospect Ave.
Estes Park, CO 80517
(970) 586-2317
https://eph.org

For emergencies call:

911

Rocky Mountain National Park Emergency Line

(970) 586-1203
Emergency call boxes are located at Wild Basin Ranger Station, Longs Peak Ranger Station, the Lawn Lake and Cow Creek trailheads, the Bear Lake parking lot, Park & Ride, and in the backcountry at the intersection of the Twin Owls and Gem Lake Trails.

Index